Robert D. Nye is Associate Professor of Psychology at the State University College, New Paltz, New York. He received B.A. and Ph.D. degrees from George Washington University, where he was elected to Phi Beta Kappa. His previous books are *Conflict Among Humans* and *Three Views of Man: Perspectives from Sigmund Freud, B.F. Skinner, and Carl Rogers.*

WHAT IS
B.F. SKINNER
REALLY SAYING?

Robert D. Nye

S-630 $4.95

A SPECTRUM BOOK

PRENTICE-HALL, INC., Englewood Cliffs, N. J. 07632

Library of Congress Cataloging in Publication Data

Nye, Robert D.
    What is B. F. Skinner really saying?

    (A Spectrum Book)
    Includes bibliographical references and index.
    1. Skinner, Burrhus Frederic, 1904-
2. Operant conditioning. 3. Psychology—Philosophy.
I. Title.
BF319.5.06N93   150'.19'4340924   79-21254
ISBN 0-13-952192-5
ISBN 0-13-952184-4

To EILEEN, for many reasons

A SPECTRUM BOOK

10   9   8   7   6   5   4   3   2   1

Printed in the United States of America

PRENTICE-HALL INTERNATIONAL, INC., *London*
PRENTICE-HALL OF AUSTRALIA PTY. LIMITED, *Sydney*
PRENTICE-HALL OF CANADA, LTD., *Toronto*
PRENTICE-HALL OF INDIA PRIVATE LIMITED, *New Delhi*
PRENTICE-HALL OF JAPAN, INC., *Tokyo*
PRENTICE-HALL OF SOUTHEAST ASIA PTE. LTD., *Singapore*
WHITEHALL BOOKS LIMITED, *Wellington, New Zealand*

ACKNOWLEDGMENTS

Without the research and writings of B. F. Skinner, this book obviously would not have been written. I appreciate his effects on me and am thankful for the "inspiration" that resulted from reading his articles and books.

Eileen Campbell again provided support and suggestions, as she did during my previous writing projects. She has always been willing to help, and I am grateful.

Several other persons also were specially involved. Two of my teaching colleagues, Mark Sherman and Richard Sloan, read and commented on portions of the manuscript. Dr. Sherman's knowledge of behaviorism and Dr. Sloan's nonbehavioristic perspectives were valuable to me. A psychology major and friend, Rose Mastrovito, contributed her comments and helped sustain my optimism. Larry Wrightsman, of the University of Kansas, provided encouragement during an early stage of my work on this project, and I thank him for helping to make it seem sensible and worthwhile.

Robert Epstein and Fred Keller served as reviewers of the manuscript. Both have been closely associated with Skinner and his work, and I benefited greatly from their helpful suggestions, detailed advice, and enthusiasm. Responsibility for the content and accuracy of the final copy, however rests with me.

Judy Bufano, Colleen Ellmore, and Marie Jourard typed the manuscript with no complaints and lots of smiles, which I needed.

CONTENTS

TEN
CONCLUDING COMMENTS

INDEX

ONE

INTRODUCTION: THIS BOOK AND HOW IT GREW

B. F. Skinner and the radical behaviorism that he advocates are very controversial. He has a large and loyal following, but he also has many opponents who enthusiastically counter his views. There are individuals in both the pro- and anti-Skinner camps who have presented well-informed arguments and perspectives. Still, for many people there remain misunderstandings and misinterpretations about what Skinner is *really* saying. This book is an attempt to help those who are interested (whether laypersons, students, or professionals) gain a clear understanding of Skinner's basic behavioral concepts and his various ideas. It is based on the belief that Skinner's approach, right or wrong, is lively, timely, and provides a real challenge to some of our traditional ways of thinking about human behavior.

The mere mention of the name "Skinner" or the term "behaviorism" can arouse strong emotional responses, which are often accompanied by comments such as:

"Skinner? Oh, yes, he's the one who thinks people are like rats in mazes."

"Skinner believes that people are robots."

"There's no place for individualism in Skinner's scheme of things."

"If Skinner has his way, we'll all be controlled like puppets by some mastermind who pulls our strings."

"Skinner doesn't take human feelings and emotions into account; he's too coldblooded. Besides, he says that there are no such things as freedom and dignity."

These statements don't accurately represent Skinner's views. Indeed, some of them contain a note of fear or suspicion that can detract from careful consideration of the meanings and possible importance of his proposals, as in the following comment: "Skinner talks about control and says we all are controlled by external conditions. That's enough for me. I'm not interested in controlling or being controlled. I'm interested in being myself and in being free and that's what I want to know about."

Probably Skinner's rapidly growing public reputation is due in part to the very misinterpretations, oversimplifications, and suspicions that exist. They make his ideas more sensational. Unfortunately, the real nature of his proposals often remains distorted and their potential benefits are overlooked. With all of the personal and social problems that we face, it seems ill advised to ignore suggestions that might lead to the betterment of our troublesome situations. A closer and clearer look at the actual content of Skinner's proposals is needed to see what potential benefits exist.

My own position with regard to Skinner's radical behaviorism is this: I'm not a completely devoted disciple, but much of what he says makes good sense to me. As I've become more familiar with his writings, I've become increasingly friendly toward his views. My initial reactions to Skinner, after first hearing about him many years ago, were similar to the reactions of many others. I thought his ideas about human behavior were simplistic, that they had only very limited application, and that they were somewhat depressing in their emphasis on how we are controlled by our surrounding conditions. I was much more interested in theories that emphasize the importance of our feelings, thoughts, and expectations as determinants of what we do. Even after I had been a college teacher for several years, and had developed a course comparing Skinner with several other major figures in psychology, I considered his approach rather sterile. I devoted a substantial part of the course to his ideas and concepts of behavior mainly because of their importance within the field of psychology. Additionally, I felt it was fun and instructive to compare his approach with other influential psychological theories (psychoanalysis, for example).

As the years went by, I continued teaching this course. I read more of Skinner's writings, as well as those of other theorists. Time and again I reviewed these writings as I attempted to respond clearly and specifically to students' questions. Also I began writing a book which eventually was published in 1975: *Three Views of Man: Perspectives from Sigmund Freud, B. F. Skinner, and Carl Rogers*.[1] (Rogers is a major figure in humanistic psychology; he is best known as the founder of client-centered therapy, a humanistically oriented therapeutic approach.) In concise form I presented the major ideas of these three influential men and then compared, contrasted, and criticized them. It was an interesting experience. As I became involved with each theorist, I found myself "taken over" by that particular view of human behavior. Only after I had finished writing the book did I feel that I could step back and look at each approach objectively.

My thinking about Skinnerian psychology has changed over the years. Intensive exposure to this approach, while simultaneously studying alternative approaches, has resulted in an increased appreciation of Skinner's concepts. Contrary to my initial impression many years ago, they seem to apply to a wide variety of human situations. Also contrary to some of my earlier feelings, Skinner's ideas now strike me as being quite optimistic—they give cause for hope that we can solve some of the difficulties that plague our society and ourselves.

In short, two major thoughts accompanied the writing of this book: a growing sense of the importance of Skinner's work and the awareness that his ideas are often misjudged. I believe that a clear, concise picture of what Skinner has said in various writings is necessary, so that individuals can decide for themselves whether or not the Skinnerian approach has value. In addition to providing such an overview, this book gives a solid basis for comparing Skinner's concepts with those of other thinkers in the field of psychology, and for judging the discussions and comments that currently abound regarding him and his approach. He is discussed not only in psychology textbooks and college courses, but also in popular magazines such as *Time*, *Newsweek*, and *Playboy*, and on

---

[1]Robert D. Nye, *Three Views of Man: Perspectives from Sigmund Freud, B. F. Skinner, and Carl Rogers* (Monterey, Ca.: Brooks/Cole Publishing Company, 1975.)

TV talk shows (Skinner himself appeared on Dick Cavett's show and on William Buckley's "Firing Line," as well as on other shows). He comes up in cocktail party conversations, PTA meetings, friendly philosophical debates, and practically anywhere that ideas are exchanged.

A question that might be asked at this point is: "If someone wants to learn what Skinner really has to say, why not simply read his writings?" My answer is: "That would be great, but . . . ." The main qualifications that I would add are: (1) Skinner's ideas appear in a large number of articles, books, and published talks, and therefore it isn't easy to "simply read his writings," and (2) he sometimes discusses complex behavioral concepts and issues, such as the role of feelings in a behavioristic analysis, that are difficult to understand without some preparation (the present book helps provide this preparation).

My intention is to inform readers about B. F. Skinner and his approach in a *relatively* quick and easy (but accurate) way. If some who would not have done so otherwise are stimulated to read Skinner's own works, I will be doubly pleased. The material that follows consists of my interpretations of his writings after years of careful study. In various places I've inserted my own examples and have expanded on his statements. I believe that these additions help clarify his concepts and provide an accurate picture of important aspects of Skinnerian psychology.

It must be remembered, however, in fairness to the originator, that the final authority on what B. F. Skinner is really saying is Skinner himself. Also, it should be realized that a good deal more has been said in his many years of writing that could possibly be included in this book. Whenever you want to know *exactly* how he has been said in his many years of writing than could possibly be is no substitute for consulting his original writings. For readers who intend to pursue Skinner's own works, this book can serve as an introduction and can highlight certain topics. For those who already have read some of his writings, it may provide clarification, promote reflection, and encourage further reading.

The chapters are arranged in a sequence that seems logical to me. However, they can actually be read in any sequence, depending on the reader's interests and "reading style." Some people prefer to go directly to the subjects that interest them most. The chapters stand independently, that is, each is complete on its own. I do believe that for the fullest appreciation and understanding of the material, especially for the person who has little or no prior exposure to Skinnerian psychology, the chapter sequence makes sense. However, for those who want to "ramble around" among the chapters, there aren't any serious disadvantages.

TWO

WHO IS
B. F. SKINNER?

Skinner's name is widely recognized. In a recent study, 82 percent of college students could identify him.[1] But does that mean that they really know about the man and his background? Probably not. The following information fills in some of the details of Skinner's life. Knowing something about a person helps to put his ideas into a proper context.

Burrhus Frederic Skinner ("Fred" to his friends) was born on March 20, 1904, in Susquehanna, a small railroad town in northeastern Pennsylvania. His mother had trouble with the birth and almost died (this was occasionally brought to Skinner's attention during the following years). His first name came from his mother's maiden name (it has been a problem for him because of the necessity of spelling and explaining it). His father was William Arthur Skinner, an attorney with political aspirations who worked for the Erie Railroad for some time; his mother was Grace Madge Skinner, a woman whom Skinner has described as being "bright and beautiful," with strict, unchanging standards.[2]

Physical punishment was hardly a part of Skinner's upbringing. His father never used it and his mother applied it only once, washing his mouth out with soap for using a bad word. Though reluctant to use physical force, it seems that his parents

[1] This finding is from Rae Goodell, "The Visible Scientists," a doctoral dissertation reported in *APA Monitor* (Washington, D. C.: American Psychological Association), August 1975, pp. 1, 8.

[2] Unless otherwise noted, all quotations in this chapter are from B. F. Skinner's autobiography in *A History of Psychology in Autobiography* (vol. 5). Ed. by E. G. Boring and G. Lindzey. New York: Irvington Publishers, Inc., 1967, pp. 387–413. Other informative and interesting sources of information are Skinner's *Particulars of My Life*, New York: Alfred A. Knopf, 1976, and *The Shaping of a Behaviorist*, New York: Alfred A. Knopf, 1979.

were not as hesitant in using other methods to bring home the importance of good behavior. William Skinner often told his son about the consequences of having a "criminal mind" and even went so far as to take young Skinner to the county jail to impress him with the facilities there. Also, during one of his summer vacations, the boy was taken to a lecture in which life at Sing Sing Prison was described using color slides (Skinner admits that even today he has a fear of the police). Apparently the importance of such demonstrations was also believed in by Grandmother Skinner, who pointed out to the boy the similarities between hell and the glowing coals in the parlor stove.

Skinner's mother was very concerned with proper behavior and with what other people might think. A second-grade report card of Skinner's, on which the phrase "Annoys others" was checked in the deportment section, and was the cause of considerable upset in the family. He says that he is still haunted by notions of things that are "right"; one example is his "twinge" when cracking the spine of a book—the effects of being taught to "respect books" are still with him.

Skinner's early life seems to have been quite secure and, in many ways, ideally representative of an all-American small-town boyhood of an earlier time. He has described his home environment as "warm and stable." His grandparents, whom he saw frequently, provided influences in addition to those exerted by his parents. He lived in the same house from birth until just before he left for college (when the family moved to Scranton, Pennsylvania) and attended the high school from which his parents had graduated. It was a small school, having all twelve grades in the same building; there were eight students in Skinner's graduating class. He enjoyed school and got a strong grounding in mathematics, Latin, science, and English. He was used to being around books, since his father had a tendency to be "a sucker for book salesman," as Skinner has put it. Outside of his school activities, he enjoyed wandering through the hills around Susquehanna and did the usual things a boy would do in such a setting: swam in the creek, ate berries, killed rattlesnakes, canoed down the river with other boys, and so on. Young Skinner also had a penchant for building and inventing. He built sleds, rafts, bows and arrows, blow guns, roller-skate scooters, wagons, model airplanes, and more; a favorite project was to try to build a glider in which to fly. His inventions included a flotation system for separating ripe from green elderberries and a perpetual motion machine that didn't work. Skinner also had musical and artistic interests, playing the saxophone and piano quite well and doing watercolors and charcoal drawings. (Even today, a piano, an organ, and a clavichord can be found in his home.)

A strong influence on Skinner during his school days was an unmarried teacher named Mary Graves. She had strong cultural interests and was the organizer of a local literary club, the Monday Club, to which Skinner's mother belonged. Miss Graves was Skinner's teacher in a number of classes, including drawing in the lower grades and English later on. She also taught Presbyterian Sunday School classes, and took Skinner and a number of other boys through most of the Old Testament. (Skinner's religious training, apparently begun by his grandmother, spanned the years of his early youth, but while still in his teens he became disenchanted with his belief in God.)

A disagreement with Miss Graves about whether or not Shakespeare had actually written As You Like It stimulated Skinner, in the eighth grade, to rush to the library and search through various sources to defend the notion that Francis Bacon actually was the author. This undertaking was probably his first real taste of dedicated scholarship. Skinner has suggested that it was likely Miss Graves's influence that caused him to become an English literature major in college and, after college graduation, to attempt a writing career.

The decision of where to go to college was not complicated for Skinner. A family friend suggested Hamilton College, a small liberal arts college at Clinton, New York, and that's where he went. He quickly joined a fraternity and took, as he says, "an absurd program of courses" which, despite its absurdity, he feels has been of good use to him. While majoring in English, his other courses included Romance languages, public speaking, biology, embryology, cat anatomy, and mathematics. He found that what had been considered good standard English in Susquehanna was not considered so at Hamilton, and he had some difficulties learning proper phrasings and pronunciations.

A tragedy occurred at home while Skinner was visiting from college during the Easter vacation of his freshman year. His only brother, two-and-a-half years younger, became suddenly and severely ill. The doctor was called quickly but nothing could be done. At age sixteen the boy died from a cerebral hemorrhage. This death had a dramatic effect on the family, but Skinner remained fairly objective about it. The relationship between Skinner and his brother had been noncompetitive in certain ways because of their different interests, but the younger brother had been better at sports, was more popular, and was closer to their parents. As occurs in most families, there was teasing between the brothers, with the older Skinner being the recipient of remarks about his artistic and literary interests. With his brother gone, Skinner became the focus of increased attention within the family and this position was uncomfortable for him.

During his sophomore year, Skinner met the family of Percy Saunders, the dean of Hamilton College. He was asked to tutor one of Saunders's children in mathematics and this led to his participation in cultural activities with the family, such as musical events in their home. He admired the ability of the Saunders to make "an art of living." Through this family he met a young woman who was the daughter of a Utica, New York, banker. He developed a strong infatuation, but the feeling was not mutual and he experienced months of pain and loneliness. His meeting of the Saunders's family (and, I assume, the related developments) has been referred to by Skinner as the most important thing that happened to him at Hamilton College.

During his senior year at Hamilton, Skinner's sexual initiation took place when he and two friends (at their suggestion) visited a house of prostitution in Utica. He has suggested that the experience was brief and not as exciting as he had anticipated (probably because he was hardly at ease in the situation). There were at least two additional occasions on which he and his friends traveled to Utica for the same purpose.

Fitting comfortably into the routine of college life apparently was not Skinner's style, judging from a number of incidents about which he has written. He had difficulties adjusting to the physical education requirements because of his lack of ability at sports and complained about the injustice of such requirements. He and another student pulled off a hoax involving a supposed visit to the campus by Charles Chaplin; a large crowd (in some 400 cars) gathered in vain at the college to hear the famous actor. Skinner used student publications to attack Phi Beta Kappa (the esteemed national honorary society) and various faculty members. Even Commencement Day was considered fair game, and Skinner and his cronies made such a disturbance during their graduation ceremonies that the college president apparently threatened to refuse them their degrees. They must have settled down sufficiently to satisfy the president that to deny them their degrees would have been overly harsh punishment, because Skinner did in fact finally graduate from Hamilton College in the spring of 1926.

During the last term of his senior year, Skinner struggled with the difficult decision of what to do after college. He suggested to his parents that he return to live with them in Scranton, Pennsylvania (where they had moved the year he left for college) and write a novel using that town as the setting for the story. William Skinner responded to his son in a lengthy letter, pointing out the importance of deciding how to make a living and establishing oneself in order to be able to have a home and family of one's own. The father did not totally discourage the son's writing ambitions but gave the usual parental advice about the need to plan for the future. Whatever deterring effect this letter may have had on Skinner's plan to become a writer of fiction was quickly offset by another letter received a short time later. It was from Robert Frost, the noted poet, whom Skinner had met briefly the previous year at the Summer School of English at Bread Loaf, in Vermont. Frost had suggested that Skinner send him some of his work, and he complied by sending three short stories. Frost's response, which came in April of Skinner's last college term, was very favorable. With this push, a writing career was decided upon. After graduation Skinner moved back home and set up a study on the third floor of his family's house.

The first year during which he tried to become a writer has been referred to by Skinner as "disastrous." He thought that a novel was too large an undertaking, so he tried writing short stories—with little success. Very shortly he began feeling that his decision to write was a bad one, and he found that he was distracted easily. He began to be aware of the drabness of his life in Scranton, though he did enjoy reading, attending an occasional concert, working in a local drama group, and so on. He also started thinking about alternatives to writing: chicken farming in California, being a chauffeur, and landscape architecture. The last of these he considered after working for a landscape gardener as a laborer for thirty-five cents an hour; the plan was scrapped, however, when he discovered that he had developed a severe allergy to grass.

Finally, Skinner did manage to get a substantial writing project underway, though it was hardly what he had originally planned. His father suggested to him that he write a digest of the decisions that had been reached by the Board of Conciliation (set up by President Theodore Roosevelt) in its settlements of hundreds of grievances brought by coal companies and unions. The purpose of the digest would be to provide company lawyers with a convenient reference. Skinner tackled the job and found it boring, but it did have its rewards. It gave him experience in classifying facts, and the money he made on *A Digest of Decisions of the Anthracite Board of Conciliation* gave him the opportunity to consider new avenues of activity. (This project gave strong evidence of how Skinner could persevere: He read and summarized 1148 grievances. He showed this tendency again in his later dogged pursuit of behavioral principles in the experimental laboratory, though in the latter case he certainly had more interest in his work.)

When it became obvious to Skinner that he had failed to become the kind of writer that he wanted to be, he attributed his failure to the literary method itself. He had wanted to investigate human behavior in his writing, but now felt that even though a writer could get down the details of behavior, he didn't necessarily understand the behavior. Following a comment made to him by an artist acquaintance, Alf Evers—"Science is the art of the twentieth century"—Skinner decided to turn his attention toward psychology, a field about which he knew almost nothing. In college he had had only the barest exposure to psychology, though some of his reading did border on it. After beginning to seriously consider psychology as the discipline that he would pursue, Skinner's reading focused more directly on that field. Bertrand Russell's book *Philosophy* came to his attention. In this book, Russell spent considerable time on the behavioristic approach of John B. Watson (the founder of behaviorism); though not in fundamental agreement with Watson, Russell nevertheless suggested that there was a good deal of truth in his proposals. This inspired Skinner to buy Watson's book *Behaviorism*, and he moved from a philosophical approach to psychology toward an empirical, scientific approach.

The final confirmation of Skinner's decision to turn from literature to psychology resulted from his reading of an article by H. G. Wells, published in 1927 in the *New York Times Magazine*, in which Wells expressed his admiration for the work of Ivan Pavlov (the famous Russian physiologist who studied conditioned reflexes and thereby made a tremendous contribution to scientific psychology). Thoroughly convinced of his desire to study psychology, Skinner began inquiring about graduate schools. He finally applied for admission to Harvard University, and was accepted for the fall of 1928.

Skinner has said that his decision to go into psychology was determined by "many odds and ends." Certainly the events mentioned in the previous paragraph were important, but earlier occurrences also played a part. During his youth, he was impressed by the performing pigeons at a county fair, and he always had been interested in animal behavior: for example, he had captured and observed turtles, snakes, chipmunks, lizards, and toads. His father had perhaps stimulated his interest in psychology by frequently calling his attention to interesting bits of behavior, such as the methods baseball players use to deceive the umpire and the unique speech patterns of certain people. Even at an early age, Skinner was curious about any unusual behaviors that he saw. At least some of the roots of his interest in psychology clearly extended back to his experiences as a youngster.

Skinner's acceptance for graduate study at Harvard greatly pleased his parents, and his father suggested that the family take a European trip during the coming summer. Skinner was not overjoyed at the thought of traveling with his parents, but he agreed to go, with the qualification that he would arrive ahead of them and spend a month or two on his own. That still gave him several months before leaving, and he decided to spend the time in Greenwich Village in New York. He had acquaintances there and he knew something about it from a previous visit. During the months that he spent in the Village before leaving for Europe, Skinner read more psychology (including Pavlov's *Conditioned Reflexes* and Watson's *Psychological Care of Infant and Child*), went to parties, had an affair with a married woman, and worked in a bookstore for fifteen dollars a week. The time to go to Europe arrived, and it went as planned: He went ahead of his parents, did some traveling, and met them in Paris. More traveling followed and then they returned to Scranton. Shortly after, Skinner headed for Cambridge, Massachusetts, and Harvard University.

About his early experiences at Harvard, Skinner has written that his interests initially were a "hodgepodge," and that the department of psychology had little effect on his sorting out of these interests. Two fellow graduate students, Fred Keller and Charles Trueblood, helped him do that. Keller already was a dedicated behaviorist and Trueblood (who, like Skinner, previously had been involved in writing) was studying the behavior of rats in mazes. Among Skinner's studies were psychophysical methods, abnormal psychology, statistics, and German (to satisfy the language requirement). He says that the intellectual life that surrounded him at the department of psychology "was of a high order" and he had the chance to interact with influential thinkers not only in psychology, but also in related fields. In the fall of 1930, Skinner wrote his doctoral thesis, a study of reflex behavior, and received his Ph.D. the following year.

Skinner stayed on at Harvard for five years after finishing his doctoral work, being supported by fellowships as he did various animal studies. His approach was heavily influenced by Pavlov: He followed the principle of "control the environment and you will see order in behavior."

When Skinner's fellowship ended in 1936, the country was in the midst of a severe economic depression. Job prospects looked bleak, but through personal contacts Skinner was offered a teaching position at the University of Minnesota for a salary of nineteen hundred dollars. He had never taught before and felt that he was keeping only a small jump ahead of his students in introductory psychology. However, he did a very effective job: Five percent of his students over a five-year period went on to get Ph.D.s in psychology. He says of this experience that he has "never again been so richly reinforced as a teacher."

In 1936 another important event occurred. Skinner married Yvonne Blue, a former English major from the University of Chicago. They had met through mutual friends only about six weeks before their marriage. According to an article on Skinner that appeared in *Time* magazine (September 20, 1971), she remembers her reaction: "When I met him, he was convinced he was a genius." Yvonne Skinner shares her husband's strong interest in reading, though he admits that "she reads exactly twice as fast as I."

The Skinners have two children. The first, Julie, is a professor of educational psychology, has written textbooks in that field, and is married to a sociologist. The second, Deborah, has been the subject of much public attention and concern. When the Skinners decided to have their second child, Yvonne commented that she felt the first two years of childrearing are difficult. Her husband responded by suggesting that they mechanize some of the required care of the baby. Thus, the "aircrib" (originally referred to by Skinner as the "baby-tender") was born, along with Deborah Skinner, and she became the famous "baby in a box." Skinner published an article in 1945 in the *Ladies' Home Journal*, reporting on the aircrib and the progress of his infant daughter.[3]

The special crib consisted of an enclosed space with a glass front, through which the baby could watch what was going on around her. Because of the carefully regulated temperature within the enclosure, she only had to wear a diaper; the usual undershirt, nightdress, sheets and blankets were unnecessary. This was a real benefit because it gave more freedom of movement to the infant and also prevented the development of rashes (it also cut down on the amount of laundry and the continual dressing and undressing that usually must be done). The floor of the aircrib was covered with a tightly stretched woven plastic sheet, with a texture similar to linen. This sheet was about ten yards long, wrapped on a spool at one end of the crib and emptying into a hamper on the other; this allowed the sheet to be pulled through as it became soiled, a convenient way of providing a consistently clean surface for the baby to lie on. The aircrib was partially soundproofed, and a shade could be drawn over the glass front.

Despite the fact that Skinner tried to make it clear that there were obvious advantages to using the aircrib, many people were alarmed by what they considered a cold, unfeeling method of handling (or, rather, *not* handling) an infant. It is true that Deborah immediately went into the aircrib after she was brought home from the hospital and used it for two-and-a-half years as a sleeping space, *but* it must be remembered that she was able to see out through the glass whenever she was active *and*, very importantly, she was taken out frequently for play and cuddling. She was by no means simply stuck into the crib and forgotten. Even today, however, despite the fact that hundreds of parents

[3]More recently, another account by Skinner of the aircrib has appeared in a popular magazine. See "My Experience with the Baby-Tender," *Psychology Today*, March 1979, pp. 29– 40.

(including Skinner's older daughter) have used aircribs, rumors persist that Skinner was inhumane and uncaring toward Deborah. Furthermore, it is often suggested that she is either psychotic and institutionalized or has committed suicide. (At least once during each semester that I teach, I have to respond to a question something like: "How does Skinner feel about the daughter who went crazy after being kept in a box?" or "Isn't it true that one of Skinner's daughters is psychotic and that the other committed suicide?")

Though a lot of suspicion exists about the outcomes of Skinner's "baby box" procedure, it seems ill-founded. Deborah went to college, studied art in London, and has established herself in that field (one showing of her colored etchings was conducted under the auspices of the Royal Academy of Arts). Also, she is married, is interested in a wide variety of music, and can beat her father at chess. (She did break her leg while skiing, but Skinner has disavowed responsibility for that.) Deborah herself has suggested that probably the rumors about her, rather than the aircrib experience, are responsible for any psychological problems that she has had. In the *Time* article referred to earlier, she indicated her belief that criticisms of the aircrib are based on misunderstandings, and that as a baby she was very happy.

To get back to Skinner's career, he stayed at the University of Minnesota from 1936 to 1945. His first major work, *The Behavior of Organisms*, was published in 1938 and reported his research with rats. His famous novel, *Walden Two*, was written during the summer of 1945 (it was not published until 1948; he had difficulty finding an interested publisher). Skinner had accepted a position, starting in the fall of 1945, as professor and chairman of the department of psychology at Indiana University and therefore had only a short time left in Minneapolis. He felt a variety of dissatisfactions that summer regarding certain common life problems: He wondered whether there could be a better way to deal with situations such as running a household, educating children, finding leisure time to enjoy one's hobbies, and being able to do the kind of work that one finds most satisfying. It seems that having to leave the security of his life in Minnesota to take over the responsibilities of a chairmanship at Indiana University played a part in stimulating Skinner to think about these matters. This move involved uprooting his oldest daughter from her school, finding new housing, leaving friends behind, and so forth. These types of considerations led him to write *Walden Two*, a fictional attempt to portray a society in which many everyday problems are solved in nontraditional ways. In *The Behavior of Organisms*, Skinner had not attempted to apply his laboratory results to the outside world; in *Walden Two* this is precisely what he did attempt to do. It is a story of a community that is run according to principles of behavioral engineering, and of a small group of outsiders who visit the community.

Skinner has said that writing *Walden Two* was "a venture in self-therapy" in which he was trying to reconcile inconsistencies in his own behavior. On the one hand, Skinner was pursuing a rewarding, but traditional, academic and scientific career, but there was a part of him that leaned toward accepting a different approach to life, one that would involve turning his back on the university to try a new, communal-type lifestyle as pictured in *Walden Two*. The university won out, apparently because Skinner was unwilling to give up his responsibilities and opportunities to advance behavioral science in the ways that he already had begun. (If he had decided otherwise, he may have had to go off to his new life alone. According to comments printed in *Time*, Yvonne Skinner was not in favor of giving up what they had to start a communal existence: "We had tremendous arguments about *Walden Two*. I wouldn't like it; I just like change and privacy."

Walden Two was written in a manner different from Skinner's usual approach. He says that he generally writes "very slowly and in longhand," producing about one hundred words that are publishable for each three or four hours of daily writing. He finished *Walden Two* in seven weeks using a typewriter, sometimes writing very emotionally. He has mentioned that one part was typed "in white heat."

After his flurry of activity on *Walden Two*, Skinner arrived at

Indiana University to assume the psychology chairmanship. His administrative duties didn't keep him out of the laboratory, as he had feared might happen. He managed to find time to do a number of behavioral experiments, using pigeons as subjects. In 1947, while giving some special lectures at Harvard University, Skinner was invited to become a permanent member of the department of psychology there. After finishing up his responsibilities at Indiana in 1948, he went back to Harvard. He has been there ever since, working consistently and amassing a long list of accomplishments that include: very successful laboratory research during the 1950s and early 1960s; many years of effective teaching; the development of teaching machines and methods of programmed instruction; the study of psychotic behavior at the Metropolitan State Hospital in Waltham, Massachusetts; and the writing of a number of significant books and articles on behavioral principles and the application of these principles to social problems.

Among the many colleges and universities that have acknowledged Skinner's contributions by awarding him honorary degrees are: Hamilton College (his alma mater), University of Chicago, University of Exeter (England), McGill University (Canada), Tufts University, Ohio Wesleyan University, and Western Michigan University. Among his numerous other distinctions are: the Distinguished Scientific Contribution Award of the American Psychological Association (1958); the National Medal of Science (1968); the International Award of the Joseph P. Kennedy, Jr., Foundation for Mental Retardation (1971); the Humanist of the Year Award, American Humanist Society (1972); and the Award for Distinguished Contributions to Educational Research and Development, American Educational Research Association (1978).

THREE

WHAT ARE THE BASIC CONCEPTS OF SKINNERIAN PSYCHOLOGY?

This chapter is the longest in the book. It should be, since Skinner's proposals for coping with human problems come from his basic concepts of behavior. They provide the foundation on which he builds. This material will enhance the understanding and appreciation of later chapters, especially for readers who are not familiar with the basics of Skinnerian psychology.

FUNDAMENTAL PREMISES

Boiling Skinnerian psychology down to its most fundamental premises, we have: (1) organisms, animal and human, are active—they emit behaviors of various kinds; (2) when a behavior is emitted it has consequences that may affect the future of the behavior—these consequences may either increase or decrease the likelihood that the behavior will occur again; (3) the consequences are determined by the organism's physical and social environments.

Skinner has filled in many details around these simple propositions and told us how various consequences affect our behaviors. He believes that this type of information is essential for understanding why people behave as they do. Though many students of human behavior prefer to look at "the inner person" to find answers to complex human activities, Skinner focuses on observable events in the external environment.

UNDERLYING ASSUMPTIONS

Beyond the simple premises stated above, there are a number of assumptions that Skinner has made in developing his psychology. These will be discussed briefly before moving on to his major behavioral concepts. They constitute a framework characterized by *objectivity, determinism,* and *a concern about practical applications.*

1. *Behavior is lawful; it is determined and controlled in systematic and consistent ways by genetic and environmental factors.*

2. *Genetic endowment determines certain aspects of behavior (for example, the basic types of behavior that we are capable of emitting); however, environmental factors determine the many details of behavior and can be observed and altered more directly.* Even though we inherit certain capabilities and potentials, it is the environmental experiences of each of us that shape and maintain the specific behaviors that characterize us as individuals. Also, environmental factors are easier to observe and to change than are genetic factors. (A distinction sometimes is made between "genetic" and "environmental" as though the former is completely separate from the latter. It must be remembered, however, that Darwin's theory of evolution suggests that genetic endowment is determined by environmental conditions. The species members who behave in ways that allow survival in their environments are the ones most likely to produce offspring, thereby perpetuating their particular genetic—and behavioral—characteristics. Skinner points out the importance of past environments in selecting behaviors by referring to "contingencies of survival.")

3. *The role of psychology is to discover the "cause-and-effect" relationships between environmental factors and behavior.* (To be precise, cause-and-effect connections in scientific

studies are commonly referred to as "functional relations." Though scientists may reveal the effect that one event has on another, they are cautious about implying that they know *how* the event causes its effect. Therefore, Skinner considers the phrase "functional relations" to be appropriate. He suggests, however, that the terms "cause" and "effect" can be used informally.) The field of psychology has the special task of investigating the effects of environmental factors on behavior. Other scientists, such as those involved in studying physiology, eventually may be able to tell us specifically what occurs inside the body when we behave. This will be valuable information. However, since knowledge of the relationships between environmental factors and behavior always will be crucial, psychologists should vigorously pursue their own speciality.

4. *The best method for determining critical relationships is to control specific environmental conditions ("causes") and observe the resulting behavioral outcomes ("effects").* This is the "experimental method," and is quite different from the kinds of observations that we make in everyday life (which are usually "uncontrolled" observations, meaning that all sorts of unknown factors can be affecting the behaviors we are looking at, thereby making it difficult or impossible to determine the critical factors). Using the experimental method, specific conditions can be arranged deliberately and the resulting changes in behavior can be observed.

5. *Studies of lower animals are useful in determining basic behavioral concepts that can then be tested out at the human level.* The main advantages of studying rats, pigeons, and other lower animals is that they are simpler than humans, their past histories and present circumstances can be controlled more easily, and they can be studied over longer periods of time under specified conditions. Though humans obviously are different from lower animals, there is no reason to reject the possibility that the same behavioral concepts

apply to both. (In fact, considerable evidence indicates that various concepts *do* apply to both.)

6. *Behavioral concepts derived from the experimental study of relationships between environmental factors and behaviors can be applied to human problems.* Findings from both animal and human studies can be used to improve human conditions. They can be brought out from psychologists' laboratories into the real world, applied to real-life situations, and monitored carefully to determine their effectiveness. (This approach has been used effectively in many cases.)

7. *It is unnecessary and misleading to speculate about feelings, thoughts, or other "inner states" as causes of behavior.* Such states certainly do occur, but these internal (bodily) conditions do not control behavior. Environmental conditions (for example, reinforcement or punishment) influence these inner responses as well as overt behaviors. In other words, they can be considered effects rather than causes. (This is perhaps the hardest aspect of Skinnerian psychology to accept, since we are so used to attributing our actions to our feelings and thoughts.)

OPERANT BEHAVIOR

Skinner is interested primarily in behaviors that have effects on the physical and social environments within which we live. He sees humans as active organisms, capable of emitting a wide variety of such behaviors. Behaviors that "operate" or act on the environment to produce consequences, and are in turn affected by these consequences, are called *operants*. The consequences determine whether we do the same thing (or something similar) again, or try something else. Certain outcomes strengthen the types of behavior that precede them while others do not. The multitude of consequences that we experience during our lifetimes shapes us into what we are at any given point in time. To use a non-Skinnerian word, these outcomes determine an individual's own unique "personality." The study of operant behavior is at the core of Skinnerian psychology, so much so that often it is referred to as "operant behaviorism." Skinner's operant behaviorism should be distinguished from earlier forms of behaviorism, such as that of John B. Watson, who is generally considered the first behaviorist in the field of psychology (his writings on the subject began to appear in 1913). Watson paid considerable attention to the findings of Ivan Pavlov, the famous Russian physiologist who gave us Pavlovian conditioning.

It is not unusual to read or hear comments which equate Skinner's and Pavlov's interests. However, they are very different. The work for which Pavlov is famous concentrated on the study of relatively simple, reflexive type responses. For example, many people have heard of the studies in which he trained dogs to salivate to the sound of a tone. After being paired repeatedly with the presentation of food, the tone by itself elicited salivation. Thus, an initially neutral stimulus (a tone) became a conditioned stimulus. The dog was relatively passive in this conditioning process. It was strapped into a harness-type apparatus, and the salivation reflex was elicited by presenting food slightly after the tone was sounded. In Skinner's studies, as you will see, more active responding is required for conditioning to occur.

The conditioning of a reflexive response (such as salivation) to an initially neutral stimulus (such as a tone) has important implications. Watson believed, and demonstrated in a very dramatic study, that emotional responses such as irrational fears can be explained by Pavlovian conditioning.[1] By pairing the presence of a white rat (an initially neutral stimulus) with a loud noise (a frightening stimulus), he conditioned an infant to fear the rat. Before it had been paired with the loud noise, the animal elicited no fear responses from the infant. (Though Watson's findings, published in 1920, are important, serious questions remain about the ethics of having conducted such research.)

[1]John B. Watson and Rosalie Rayner, "Conditioned Emotional Reactions," *Journal of Experimental Psychology*, 3, (February 1920), 1–14.

Skinner acknowledges the significance of Pavlovian conditioning (he calls it "respondent conditioning") in explaining various reflexive type responses to initially neutral stimuli, but his main interest is in the more active, voluntary type responses that organisms make. He believes that these are more important, since they make up most of the activities that we engage in, such as reading, studying, writing, playing sports, working, developing hobbies, talking to each other, and so on—none of these are primarily reflexive actions, but rather consist of *operants*. In this emphasis, Skinner differs from Watson's earlier focus on Pavlovian conditioning.

THE SKINNER BOX

To pursue his interest in operant behavior, Skinner built a small, soundproof chamber that provides an experimental space within which an animal can be studied. This type of device is commonly referred to as a *Skinner box*, though Skinner himself avoids calling it that. In this chamber an animal can be isolated from interfering influences and subjected to specific conditions created by the experimenter. The operant behaviors that typically are studied are lever pressing by a rat or the pecking of a small disk (called a "key") by a pigeon. When sufficient pressure is applied to the lever or the key, a food dispenser is triggered and a food pellet or grain (which serves as a reinforcer for lever pressing or key pecking) is made available. The animal's presses or pecks are recorded electromechanically over a space of time, with the rate of response being the datum that is of primary interest.

Various environmental conditions can be produced by an experimenter to see how each condition affects the animal's response rate. For example, how frequently does a rat press the lever if a food pellet is delivered after each response, when compared with a condition in which food appears after every 15 responses? In simple terms, such studies indicate how hard an animal will work under different conditions of reinforcement.

Another question might be, "If an animal has been trained to respond at a high rate by reinforcing its responses, how long will it take for the animal to stop responding when reinforcers are no longer available?" This can be studied by establishing a period of time during which food pellets are delivered when a rat presses or a pigeon pecks, and then cutting off the food supply until the animal "gives up" on that response. By doing innumerable studies of this kind, in which conditions are varied in specific detail, Skinner and his colleagues have collected a vast amount of data on how environmental factors affect the frequency of behaviors.

Important questions often arise when Skinner-box studies are discussed: "What do they have to do with *our* behavior?" "How can lever pressing and key pecking be related to the behaviors that *humans* engage in?" These questions can be answered in at least two ways. *First*, Skinner has looked for basic behavioral concepts, and these concepts can be discovered in their purest forms by studying organisms that are relatively simple and easy to control experimentally. The relative isolation provided by the Skinner box helps keep the situation itself simple, by ruling out all sorts of possible interfering influences on the animal's behavior. *Second*, the concepts that are discovered by studying lower animals can be tested at the human level. In other words, Skinner doesn't suggest that rats and pigeons are exactly the same as people. Rather, he believes that there are certain *similarities* among living organisms and that behavioral processes found at one level may well apply at other levels.

Once a process is known to occur with rats or pigeons in a Skinner box, we are in a position to move to more complex levels and check on its validity in the world populated by people. In fact, this is what has happened with Skinnerian procedures. Many studies have shown that they can be applied effectively in education, industry, business, government, prisons, mental institutions, and family settings. They don't always work easily or perfectly, but often they can be tailored to fit particular situations so that substantial benefits are obtained, such as increases in efficiency and productivity, better interpersonal relationships, and decreases in undesirable behaviors.

What Skinner and his colleagues have done is similar to what goes on in other sciences, such as physics, chemistry, biology, and medicine. Researchers in these fields often study phenomena in the artificial environments of their laboratories, hoping to produce findings that will apply under real-world conditions. Medical researchers, for example, often use lower animals to test drugs or procedures before applying them to humans.

A comment needs to be made regarding the use of *rates of response* as the basic data collected by Skinner and other behaviorists who have followed in his footsteps. In Skinner-box studies (as well as in studies of human behavior in real-life settings) these data allow comparisons to be made of the effects of different conditions. The actual behaviors that are counted electromechanically in the Skinner box, that is, pressing or pecking, are used simply because they are convenient to measure and they occur reliably. There is nothing especially significant about these particular responses as far as Skinnerian psychology is concerned—other responses with similar characteristics could be used. The *rate* of response, however, is more critical. Given some thought, it becomes clear that many assumptions made about both animals and people are based on the frequency with which specific behaviors occur. For example, our assumptions about someone's attitudes, interests, habits, or preferences are often based on how frequently we observe that individual do certain things. Isn't it important, then, to understand the various conditions that cause increases or decreases in what organisms do? This is what Skinner has studied.

REINFORCEMENT

The most important of Skinner's behavioral concepts is *reinforcement*. The term indicates a *strengthening effect* that occurs when operant behaviors have certain consequences. Behavior increases in probability (that is, the likelihood of its occurrence under similar circumstances increases) when its outcomes are reinforcing. A food-deprived rat, whose lever pressing in a Skinner box is reinforced with food pellets, presses the lever again and again.

Though it is common practice to substitute the term "reward" for "reinforcement," the two are *not* the same. Rewards may or may not strengthen behavior. For example, a teenager may behave contrary to his parents' wishes, despite the fact that they heap rewards (a car, money, freedom, etc.) on him. These parents are giving rewards to their son, but they aren't *reinforcing* his desirable behaviors. By Skinner's definition, reinforcement does strengthen behavior, so if whatever is being done doesn't have that effect, reinforcement cannot be said to be occurring. Although giving so-called "rewards" *may* be reinforcing, the important point is that they do not *necessarily* strengthen the behaviors they follow.

Sometimes people fault Skinner's reinforcement procedure by saying "I've tried it and it doesn't work!" The problem in such cases may relate to what has just been said: Reward, but not reinforcement, may have been used. You can't always find a "reinforcer" easily. Though money, gifts, praise, and so on, often do work as reinforcers, in some cases they do not. Something else may be necessary. For example, a parent may find that simply listening carefully to a son or daughter, or spending some leisure time together, reinforces desirable behaviors to a greater extent than does the giving of rewards. You can't always be sure what will be reinforcing, since differences sometimes exist from person to person, from behavior to behavior, and from situation to situation. You can only be sure that reinforcement is being used when the relevant behavior is being strengthened; in other words, the effects must be observed to determine whether or not reinforcement is occurring.

Getting back to the relatively simple situation of the lever-pressing rat in a Skinner box, at first glance this might seem only to provide a mildly interesting demonstration of how an animal's behavior can be controlled by reinforcing it. However, for Skinner and his followers, this simple form of operant conditioning is an elementary example of a behavioral process that applies across species and has tremendous significance for explaining human behavior. Skinner's early studies of rats provided him with findings that he guessed would apply at the human level, and subsequent research by many behavioral psychologists has given considerable support to the idea that the behavior of people, as well as pigeons and rats, is controlled by the consequences of their actions. Although we usually don't receive food pellets, our behaviors are dramatically affected by other reinforcers such as money, compliments, sex, public attention, and approval from others. Our actions also are often reinforced by the direct environmental changes they produce: Reaching for an object produces contact with it, approaching something brings us closer to it, turning toward someone makes him or her visible, and so on. Of course, the complexity of situations, behaviors, and reinforcers among humans is extremely different from that existing in a Skinner box. Nevertheless, the Skinnerian assumption (which is supported by a large amount of evidence) is that some of the most basic behavioral concepts (such as reinforcement) are the same.

An outstanding illustration of the effects of reinforcement on human behavior has been provided by the well-known writer, Isaac Asimov:

> Most people seem to fear and resent behaviorist notions. They seem to think it denies man freedom of will and makes of him merely a machine. I heard William Buckley discuss *Beyond Freedom and Dignity*, a book by B. F. Skinner, and he referred to Skinner's theories as implying "a dehumanization" of man. But does behaviorism dehumanize a man or merely *describe* a man?
>
> Frankly, I tend to accept behaviorist notions. I find the behavior of people quite predictable; and the better I know them, the more predictable I find their behavior. People sometimes surprise me, I admit, but I have the feeling that this is because I don't know enough about them and not because they are capable of free will.
>
> And, of course, my own behavior is most predictable of all; at least, to me. For instance, I respond favorably to praise. It has an extraordinary reinforcing effect on me. All my publishers and editors find this out at

once. It is their profession, of course, to study the weaknesses of writers and use those weaknesses to manipulate those writers. So they carefully begin to praise the quickness with which I complete my work; the speed with which I read galleys and prepare indexes; the cooperativeness with which I make (reasonable) revisions, and so on and so on.

All this I lap up with avidity; no one has ever handed out praise in larger servings than I can swallow. What's more, in order to get still more of it, I complete my work more quickly than ever, read galleys and do indexes with still greater speed, make *reasonable* revisions with at least a trace of a smile, and the result is that over the last six years I have averaged nine books a year.

Came the time when I was supposed to work on the introductions to these chapters. I was in New York; the editorial staff was in California. I sent off some introductions and heard nothing. Whereupon I grew sad and sulky and found that I didn't feel like doing any more. When I was nudged very politely by the editors, I wrote a long letter, saying that unless I knew that they liked those I had already written, I could do no further work. Whereupon the staff, suddenly enlightened, promptly sent me a letter telling me that my introductions were great and that everybody loved them. At once I sat down to write more. Periodically, they sent me kind words and I sent more introductions. It was very neat and efficient.

But does that mean I'm just a robot? That I have buttons that need pushing? That I point them out, that they push them, and that all is well? Well, I guess so. I like to be praised and that's what I work for. Maybe we all have our buttons, and maybe we all know where they are, and maybe we all do our best to get them pushed.

Could the behaviorists be saying that it's love that makes the world go round?[2]

The effects of reinforcement during our lifetimes molds our behaviors along certain lines. When we learn how to swim, ride a bike, throw a ball, sew, sweep a floor, drive a car, and so on, the successful (reinforced) responses are the ones we continue to make. The unsuccessful responses tend to drop away. The same process holds true for our social behaviors at work, school, and home. For example, speaking and dressing in acceptable ways brings approval from employers, teachers, parents, peers, and others. Approval, and other important social reinforcers, are very significant influences. Whether we consider physical or social activities, the effects of reinforcement are critical.

[2]CRM Staff, *Psychology Today: An Introduction*, 3rd ed., (New York: CRM/Random House, 1975), p. 68.

POSITIVE REINFORCEMENT
AND NEGATIVE REINFORCEMENT

In operant conditioning there actually are two types of reinforcement. So far, we have been discussing *positive reinforcement:* A response is strengthened by the *addition* of something to the situation. The "something" that is added is called a *positive reinforcer.* A rat pressing a lever for food pellets, a worker doing a job for money, a student studying to get good grades, a child "being good" to earn parental approval, and even a person pulling on a doorknob to open a door are all examples of the effects of positive reinforcement. The positive reinforcers are, respectively, food pellets, money, good grades, parental approval and an open door.

Behaviors are strengthened not only by positive reinforcers, however. Many actions that allow us to escape or avoid negative consequences also become part of our typical behavior patterns. When this happens, we are being conditioned by *negative reinforcement:* A response is strengthened by the *removal* of something from the situation. In such cases, the "something" that is removed is referred to as a *negative reinforcer* or *aversive stimulus* (these two phrases are synonymous). We already have seen that a hungry rat's lever-pressing can be strengthened by positively reinforcing that response with food pellets. We could also accomplish this by using negative reinforcement. If lever pressing removes a painful electrical charge (which can be a negative reinforcer or aversive stimulus), it is very likely that the rat will soon be conditioned to make that response whenever it receives a shock through the floor grid of the Skinner box.

The phrase "negative reinforcement" can be confusing, so it pays to consider it carefully. Remember, it refers to a process whereby behavior is *strengthened,* not weakened. Often it is confused with "punishment," which will be discussed shortly. Whereas negative reinforcement results in an *increase* in the probability of behavior, punishment typically acts to *suppress* behavior; this is a very important distinction.

Skinner suggests that negative reinforcement is a very influential determinant of behavior. Many examples exist: the child who does his chores to stop his parents' nagging, the parent who gives in to his child's demands in order to stop temper tantrums, the student who cuts classes to avoid a teacher's reprimands for poor performance, the wife who escapes her husband's tirades by going into the bedroom and locking the door, the driver who obeys speed limits to avoid being ticketed, the person who gets drunk to escape from stressful life situations, the person who takes aspirin to stop a headache, and so on. Nagging, temper tantrums, reprimands, tirades, speeding tickets, stressful situations, and headaches are *negative reinforcers* or *aversive stimuli* in these examples. Their removal is reinforcing, and therefore the behaviors that remove them tend to become conditioned.

In Skinner's opinion, it is unfortunate that so much of our social behavior is influenced by *negative* reinforcement. In an improved society we would be controlled more by *positive* reinforcement. In other words, instead of escaping and avoiding aversive stimuli, it would be better to be positively reinforced more of the time. A couple of examples illustrate the point. Schools have often relied on threats of failure or disciplinary actions to spur slow students to study hard, rather than teaching the subject matter clearly and in sufficiently small steps so that making progress could be reinforced. Employers have often counted on the fact that their employees will work in order to escape the negative consequences of unemployment, poverty, and deprivation, rather than attempting to provide conditions and jobs that are positively reinforcing.

A sign of an inefficient and poorly planned society, according to Skinner, is a heavy reliance on negative reinforcers to control behavior. The emphasis should be on positive reinforcement. One major reason for this is that the outcomes of positive reinforcement are more predictable than those of negative reinforcement. Undesirable behavior often gets strengthened by negative reinforcement. For example, a teacher might attempt to get a student to study harder by continually criticizing him, and the student might respond by doing more studying. If this stops the teacher's criticisms, studying will be negatively reinforced and the teacher's goal will have been achieved (the student's studying behavior is strengthened because it removes the aversive stimulus of criticism). However, less desirable outcomes are quite possible. The student might escape and avoid the teacher's criticisms by becoming a truant, rather than by studying. Another possibility is that the student might become very withdrawn and spend a lot of time daydreaming in order to cut himself off from the full impact of the criticism.

The main point of these examples is that using *negative* reinforcers such as criticism to control behavior may result in the reinforcement of unwanted behaviors. On the other hand, using *positive* reinforcers is more likely to give the desired result. There is nothing to escape or avoid in a positive-reinforcement situation. Therefore, alternative behaviors that are undesirable are less likely to be emitted and reinforced.

To summarize briefly, there are two different types of reinforcement: positive and negative. In both types, behavior is strengthened. In positive reinforcement, the consequence of behavior is the *addition* of something (a positive reinforcer) that increases the probability of the behavior. In negative reinforcement, the consequence of behavior is the *removal* of something (a negative reinforcer or aversive stimulus) that increases the probability of the behavior. Skinner advocates using positive, rather than negative, reinforcement to control behavior.

PRIMARY REINFORCERS
AND CONDITIONED REINFORCERS

Some positive reinforcers, such as food, water, and sexual contact are related to our basic biological functioning. These are called *primary reinforcers.* There also are negative reinforcers that are considered primary: electrical shocks, pin pricks, hard blows, extreme cold or heat, and so on. Both positive and negative primary reinforcers have a significant effect on how we behave. However, to understand Skinner's suggestion that a whole array of complex human behaviors can be controlled by reinforcement, it is necessary to consider *conditioned reinforcers.*

A conditioned reinforcer is a stimulus that is originally neutral but gains the power to reinforce through its pairing with one or more primary reinforcers. Let's look at a Skinner-box example. Suppose when a rat presses the lever, a light is rigged to go on when the pellet of food (a primary reinforcer) drops into the food tray. The pairing of the light with food occurs 50 to 100 times. Next, the situation is changed so that neither the light nor food appears when the lever is pressed, and gradually the rat's responses decline to a very low frequency (this process is called *extinction*). At this point, it is arranged for the light to go on again when the pressing response is made, but for the food pellets to remain undelivered. What will happen to the response rate? Will the light by itself serve as a reinforcer, causing the lever pressing to increase again? As if turns out, the lever-pressing response in such a situation does increase in frequency, showing that the originally neutral light stimulus has become a positive reinforcer—more accurately, a positive *conditioned* reinforcer. In cases when the light has not been previously paired with food, it does not have the effect of increasing the response rate.

At the human level there are innumerable examples of conditioned reinforcers. Perhaps the most dramatic is money. Money is associated with many necessities (primary reinforcers) and therefore serves as a reinforcer itself in a multitude of situations. Think of all the behaviors that are controlled by these pieces of paper or metal—there is little doubt about money's reinforcing characteristics.

Signs of affection, approval, or attention from others—which involve certain statements, facial expressions, and body movements—also provide examples of powerful conditioned reinforcers (however, the possibility exists that certain of these signs may be primary reinforcers, due to their evolutionary significance). These signs have a great influence on us, deriving from their many associations with primary reinforcers. Starting at birth, certain verbal and physical behaviors by parents consistently accompany the giving of basics such as food, liquids, warmth, and cuddling. In later life, signs of approval, affection, and attention continue to be associated with primary reinforcers, including sexual contacts. Conditioned reinforcers that are associated with more than one primary reinforcer are referred to by Skinner as *generalized reinforcers*.

Perhaps the most significant point about conditioned reinforcers, especially those that are generalized reinforcers, is that they eventually function independently in a variety of situations to control behavior. We often behave in ways that will yield money or signs of acceptance, approval, or attention from others, even when primary reinforcers are not immediately available. We often work long and hard, or change our behaviors dramatically, to keep these conditioned reinforcers coming. The miser is an extreme example; his behavior is almost completely controlled by money, even though he seldom uses it to buy primary reinforcers.

There also are *negative* conditioned reinforcers. For example, an academic grade of "F," the facial expression that we call a frown, the verbal statement "I don't like you," or the sight of a dentist's drill, may be stimuli that are aversive because of their past associations with basic deprivations or pain. We tend to behave in ways that allow escape from or avoidance of these aversive conditioned stimuli.

A discussion of reinforcers must include what Skinner believes to be another important influence on human behavior: the positive reinforcement of successfully manipulating the environment, that is, "being effective" or "being right." He has suggested that this type of reinforcement is very basic, perhaps related to the genetic makeup of the species. It seems reasonable to assume that those of our ancestors who were most effective in coping with their environments were also the most likely to survive and pass on their characteristics to later generations. Through evolution, then, members of the human species are perhaps inherently reinforced by their effective behaviors. This idea is very significant, since it suggests that much of what we do may occur partly because we simply are producing environmental changes. In other words, perhaps there doesn't have to be any direct or obvious gain in what we do, but rather our behavior may be positively reinforced by simply producing an effect. (Skinner gives the example of a baby who persistently shakes a rattle, with little to be gained except producing a small environmental change.) This may, in part, explain activities such as planting flowers, certain artistic pursuits, and sporting activities such as bowling and billiards, which we often say we are doing "just for the fun of it."

A final point to be made in this section is that it can be dangerous to assume too much about the ability of various stimuli to reinforce the behaviors of different individuals. Although certain reinforcers—such as money, words of praise, or a smile—tend to have a great deal of generality, what is reinforcing to one person may not be reinforcing to another, a reinforcer that works in one situation may not work in another, and different behaviors may require different reinforcers. Skinner indicates that a stimulus, to be considered a positive or negative reinforcer in a particular case, should be tested and its effects observed. In other words, does the stimulus actually serve to increase the frequency of the behavior that either *produces* it (in the case of positive reinforcement) or *removes* it (in the case of negative reinforcement)?

In practical applications, for example in trying to change the behavior of a child, a student, an employee, a spouse, a friend, an acquaintance, or anyone else, it is essential that the process include stimuli that are actually reinforcing, not stimuli that are simply thought to be reinforcing. If you try to reinforce a vegetarian with a steak dinner, an extremely active child with the opportunity to read a book, a beer drinker with a glass of expensive wine, or a solitary person with an invitation to a big party, you are not likely to produce the effect that you intend.

SUPERSTITIOUS BEHAVIOR

Typically, operant conditioning involves the strengthening of behavior when reinforcement is dependent on that behavior. There is an "actual" connection between response and reinforcer. Suppose, however, that an *accidental* connection occurs; that is, a reinforcer follows a response but is not dependent on that response. This also results in operant conditioning; the behavior that is strengthened by this process is referred to by Skinner as *superstitious behavior.* He believes that many human actions are "superstitious."

Using pigeons as subjects, Skinner has demonstrated the basic processes involved in the conditioning of superstitious behavior. A food-deprived bird is put into the Skinner box. The food dispenser is set to deliver food every 15 seconds, regardless of what the pigeon is doing. Notice that the delivery of food is not dependent on a particular type of behavior. Whatever the animal is doing at the time the reinforcer (food) arrives will be reinforced and therefore will be more likely to be occurring when the next reinforcer comes. In this way, a certain response pattern is built up. With this procedure Skinner has conditioned pigeons to regularly turn in circles, thrust their heads high into an upper corner of the cage, and show other unusual movements.

What do humans do that can be traced to processes similar to "accidental" reinforcement in the Skinner box? Rain dances are a classic example. The occasional accidental connection between the dancing and the occurrence of rain provides sufficient reinforcement to keep the practice going. As another example, it has been said that some ancient peoples had a special ritual to deal with eclipses, which apparently they viewed as a giant dragon's attempt to devour the sun. By creating as much noise as they possibly could, they would cause the dragon to release the sun. Assuming that this story is true, it would be an example of accidental *negative* reinforcement—the dragon's threat was an aversive stimulus that was removed (supposedly) by the response of making lots of noise.

In modern society there also are plenty of superstitions. When an athlete prepares for a performance, all sorts of peculiar movements are apt to occur regularly. Each baseball player, for example, has his own special routine when he comes to the plate: tapping the plate with the bat, hitching his pants up several times, touching the peak of the batting helmet in a certain way, and so on. Presumably the player's movements have been developed over time as they have been followed by the reinforcement of getting a hit. Recently, I noticed that a player with a good hitting streak came to bat with someone else's protective helmet. He stood fidgeting in the batter's box, stepped in to hit, stepped out again, took off the helmet several times to check it, and finally was rescued by the bat boy who had found the player's own helmet. Comforted, he smashed a solid hit to the outfield—another reinforcement for wearing that particular hat!

Many of us have superstitious ways of dealing with machines. Elaborate routines for starting our cars sometimes develop, despite the likelihood that only a couple of the things we do are really effective. We may go through the same routine regularly because these responses, at one time or another, have been accidently reinforced. Now we continue them, because "the car starts, doesn't it?" The same kind of thing can be seen in the ways we deal with finicky typewriters, TV sets, radios, door locks, electrical switches, and so on. If some behavior "works," even if it really isn't what is producing the reinforcing outcome, we tend to do it again.

Superstitious behaviors can develop in social situations too. A person who puts on a particular type of clothing or rearranges his or her hairstyle, and then has a good time at a party or other social occasion, may continue to do these things, even though other people were not reacting at all to these particular aspects of the person. Certain physical gestures and ways of speaking also can become conditioned behaviors when they are followed by rein- forcing attention from others, regardless of whether or not the attention is actually produced by these specific behaviors.

Skinner has suggested that even when full-blown superstitions do not result from accidental connections between behaviors and reinforcers, we can be affected in less dramatic ways by these events. He uses the example of finding a ten-dollar bill in the park. Walking in the park and looking down did not actually produce the money, and it certainly isn't likely that money would be found there again even if the individual went to that spot every day. Nevertheless, if money is a reinforcer for that person, it is now more likely that he or she will stroll that way and look downward exactly as was done when the money was found. The person's behavior has been changed, at least slightly.

It can be difficult at times to determine whether or not a behavior is superstitious. I have two acquaintances who respond in opposite ways to minor illnesses, aches, and pains. One of them goes to a doctor immediately and often receives some medication or medical advice that is followed by recovery. The other person does not go to the doctor, takes no medication, and does nothing special, but she also recovers shortly. Perhaps it would be unfair to call the first person superstitious, since going to the doctor is an acceptable and encouraged practice in our society (what people commonly consider superstitious depends heavily on cultural patterns). Also, it might be that going to the doctor actually is advisable for this particular individual's problems.

An area of contemporary life that is very touchy in discussions of superstitious behavior is religion. Are various religious beliefs and practices superstitious? A common response to this question probably is something like: "Yes, all except mine!" Obviously, Skinnerian psychology cannot provide a final answer here, since considerations of ultimate purposes and supreme powers take place at a different level of discourse.

OPERANT EXTINCTION

To this point, we have been discussing the strengthening of operant behaviors, that is, the ways in which responses are increased in frequency. Now we will discuss how operant behaviors are weakened, or decreased in frequency. Suppose that, repeatedly, nothing happens after a response is made. What then? In operant-conditioning terms, *extinction* occurs: the response decreases in frequency.

Consider a case in which behavior has been strengthened through reinforcement, and then reinforcement is no longer available. For example, the lever-pressing rat in a Skinner box has been conditioned because positive reinforcement (receiving food pellets) has been a consequence of its behavior. If the reinforcement no longer exists (the food dispenser is disconnected), the rat's lever pressing will eventually stop (or almost stop); that is, it will *extinguish*.

Extinction is another important concept for understanding human behavior. The often-asked questions, "Why doesn't she do that anymore?" or "Why has he stopped doing that?" often could be answered if changes in the consequences of the person's behaviors were known. The hard-working executive is likely to become "lazy" if his or her efforts no longer bring praise, promotions, or pay increases; your friendly, good-natured neighbor may no longer give you a warm smile and a big hello if you have been too busy in recent weeks to be friendly in return; you may find that you stop trying to call an acquaintance who never seems to be home to answer the phone. Each of these instances involves a lack of reinforcement for behavior, with the result that the behavior decreases in frequency. Often, the decrease occurs very slowly and it takes a long time before the behavior completely ceases. More will be said about extinction shortly.

PUNISHMENT

Another possible consequence of behavior is *punishment*. "Negative reinforcement" and "punishment" often are confused, but these two concepts are very different. Whereas negative reinforcement strengthens behavior, punishment typically suppresses behavior. Skinner suggests two ways in which a response can be punished: by *removing a positive reinforcer* or by *presenting a negative reinforcer* (aversive stimulus) as a consequence of the response.

Here is an example of how negative reinforcement and punishment differ, using electrical shock as the negative reinforcer or aversive stimulus. If a rat presses a lever to *remove* the shock, lever pressing is negatively reinforced and is strengthened. On the other hand, if pressing the lever *produces* the shock, lever pressing is punished and is likely to be suppressed. In both situations the shock is a negative reinforcer, but in the case of negative reinforcement it is *removed* and in the case of punishment it is *presented*. Some common examples of punishment in which a negative reinforcer is added as a consequence of behavior are: a child who is scolded for swearing, an employee who is reprimanded for arriving late for work, and a driver who is ticketed for illegal parking. Sometimes the physical environment provides punishment for behavior: the infant who touches a hot stove, the bicyclist who takes a painful fall for "showing off," and the jogger who tries to run too fast and pulls a muscle are all experiencing "natural" negative reinforcers, rather than social ones.

As mentioned previously, another type of punishment involves the *removal of positive reinforcers*. Children who have their allowances taken away for bad behavior, employees who have their pay reduced for arriving late, and drivers who have their licenses suspended for speeding are examples. Positive reinforcers—allowance, pay, and the right to drive—are taken away as a consequence of certain behaviors.

An interesting point about the term "punishment," as it commonly is used in our society, is that so-called punishments often do *not* suppress the undesirable behaviors at which they are aimed. Ticketed speeders often continue to speed, jailed criminals often continue their antisocial behaviors, reprimanded students often continue doing poorly, and spanked children often continue misbehaving. We deceive ourselves in many such instances by thinking that "punishing" the offenders is effective. A stricter definition of punishment would focus attention on the effects of the punishing actions. In other words, do these actions *actually* suppress undesirable behaviors? If not, does it pay to continue their use?

Skinner's view of using punishment to control behavior has been uncompromising. He has been consistently and strongly opposed to it. He believes that punishment does not have a permanent effect (unless it is extremely severe, in which case it also commonly disrupts or stops desirable, as well as undesirable, behaviors and causes fear, high anxiety, resentment, or other problems). Although punishing someone may temporarily cause him or her to stop behaving in an undesirable way, the behavior is likely to reappear, especially when the punishment is withdrawn. Therefore, it is ineffective in the long run and is an inefficient way to get rid of unwanted behaviors.

Other objections to using punishment are: (1) rather than simply stopping the undesirable behavior, punishment may result in other behaviors that are equally undesirable, such as "running away," counterattacking, or bitter complaining; (2) emotional by-products, such as fear, guilt, or shame may be produced, and these emotions may be felt whenever the person is around the punisher or the situation in which he or she was punished—for example, the harshly punished student may experience emotional distress whenever he or she is in the classroom, and this isn't conducive to learning; (3) punishment indicates only what a person should *not* do and doesn't give information about what should be done.

If there are so many negative aspects of punishment, why is it used so frequently? Skinner suggests that punishment often gives immediate, if not long-lasting, results. In other words, using punishment is likely to be reinforcing to the *punisher*. Physical or verbal abuse directed at someone who displeases us often causes their displeasing behavior to stop, even if only for a brief time. This is especially true if the person is in a subordinate position to us. Therefore, using punishment is often negatively reinforced (something aversive to the punisher is removed). To sum up, using punishment is dangerous because it's habit-forming for the punisher, is not a long-range solution, and has undesirable side effects.

AVERSIVE CONTROL

Along with his condemnation of punishment, Skinner also is against what he calls *aversive control*. Whereas punishment is designed to stop behavior, aversive control involves getting someone to do something by threatening, explicitly or implicitly, that aversive consequences will occur if he or she doesn't do as requested. In simple language, this is a case of "Do it, or else!" (The effectiveness of aversive control actually depends on negative reinforcement; the person does what is requested in order to escape or avoid the aversive stimulus of threat. However, as will be seen below, behaviors other than going along with what is expected may get reinforced.)

Skinner believes that this type of control should be avoided for some of the same reasons as punishment: Its outcomes are not as predictable as those of positive reinforcement and by-products such as hostility, apathy, anxiety, or stubbornness may develop. The spouse who is threatened with verbal or physical abuse unless he or she stays in line may remain away from home because of the negative reinforcement involved in getting away from the threats (or, if able, may launch a verbal or physical counterattack); the employee who is harassed by a tough supervisor may find it reinforcing to stay home "sick" or to get back at the supervisor by using sabotage techniques; the child who knows that any misbehavior at home will result in severe consequences may run away because of the reinforcement involved in escaping the constant threat of punishment; many more examples could be given. Instead of producing the expected behaviors—being a "good" husband or wife, working hard on the job, behaving properly at home, or whatever—attempts to use aversive control may backfire. Even when the purpose of getting someone to behave a certain way is accomplished, the person subjected to threats is apt to show negative emotional reactions, and this may be an outcome that the controller will not be pleased with for long.

Despite all the possible things that can go wrong when aversive control is used, it occurs frequently at all levels of society, from interpersonal relationships to governmental regulations. Skinner explains this disturbing fact: As with punishment, aversive control is often effective immediately. If the person or institution using it is powerful, it will usually work—*at least temporarily*—before the ill effects begin to show.

Skinner favors a shift toward greater use of positive reinforcement for long-range benefits. If a person's behavior is reinforced, he or she will do more of it without the necessity of direct or subtle threats. To go back to our previous examples, spouses are less likely to stray if at home they find enjoyable recreational activities, attention and affection, and satisfying sex; employees are likely to work harder if their efforts are given quick and direct recognition; and children are likely to behave better if their good behaviors are given attention and approval by parents. In these reinforcing ways, behaviors can be controlled more effectively than by using aversive control which relies on threats to get people to do what is expected of them. The effects of positive reinforcement may not be as immediate or as dramatic as those of either punishment or aversive control, but they are more likely to be long-lasting and less likely to generate undesirable actions and negative emotional states.

CONTROLLING PROBLEM BEHAVIORS

If Skinner opposes punishment as a way of stopping behaviors, what does he suggest? One possibility is extinction. This procedure involves ignoring unwanted behaviors. For example, a parent may simply not pay attention to a child's whining or outbursts of temper. The basic idea is to avoid providing any reinforcement for such actions. If no reinforcement is available, extinction should occur.

According to Skinner the effects of extinction are more permanent than those of punishment. Though sometimes there may be a brief recurrence (called "spontaneous recovery") of a behavior that has undergone extinction, extinguished behavior tends to remain at a low level of frequency. Unfortunately, however, the extinction process itself may produce emotional responses such as aggression or frustration. Before extinction has finally occurred, there may be vivid displays of these or other problem behaviors. (As will be indicated shortly, it pays to reinforce desirable behaviors while extinguishing undesirable ones.)

There are other difficulties as well. Skinner warns that the process may take a long time. Therefore, the undesirable behavior may have to be endured beyond the limits of the controller's patience while extinction is taking place. For example, having to put up with a number of temper tantrums (while simultaneously trying to ignore their existence) can be very difficult, even if they are gradually decreasing in frequency. Another problem is that there may be an increase in the undesirable behavior for a time immediately following the start of the extinction procedure. If a child typically has had his whining behavior reinforced by his parents' attention, when they no longer provide that attention he is apt to intensify his whining. Commonly, this will eventually taper off and the whining will then extinguish, but the temporarily intensified demands may be hard for the parents to put up with and they may be very tempted to give in.

Another disadvantage of extinction is that it cannot be applied easily when undesirable behavior results in harm to the person himself or to others. For example, extremely aggressive behavior cannot simply be ignored; something must be done to prevent it from occurring. Further, there must be sufficient control over the entire situation to prevent other persons from reinforcing the behavior that you are trying to extinguish. To use the example of the whining child again, an extinction procedure won't be effective if a relative, neighbor, or friend continues to respond to the child's unpleasant behavior.

Skinner admits that he doesn't have all the answers about how to cope with annoying, dangerous, destructive, or otherwise harmful activities. However, he does have a suggestion that can be applied in cases when simple extinction is not likely to be effective. He advises using a method that reinforces *incompatible* behavior. If a behavior that is incompatible with the problem behavior can be conditioned through the use of positive reinforcement, it is likely to replace the problem behavior. For example, in addition to trying to ignore a child's whining and temper tantrums, the parents should make sure that they pay attention to the child whenever he is more reasonable in his demands. In this way, they may be able to shape up more polite and cooperative behaviors. If they are successful, these more desirable responses will become the typical behaviors of the child, replacing the whining and temper tantrums.

This method of extinction combined with reinforcement of incompatible behaviors is an important procedure for use in prisons, delinquent homes, and other institutions to which serious offenders are sent for rehabilitation. Though good programs presently are in extreme shortage, this method has strong possibilities. The basic idea is to set up the situation so that no reinforcements are available for the criminal or delinquent activities that have become typical response patterns for the offenders, while providing positive reinforcement for constructive behaviors such as learning job skills, studying, and communicating better with others.

Implementing such programs is much easier said than done. One of the obvious difficulties is getting rid of the possibilities of reinforcement for undesirable behaviors such as fighting, the use and selling of drugs, and sexual attacks. Unless there is sufficient control over the total situation, such activities are likely to continue. On the other hand, complete control may be oppressive and defeat the rehabilitation process. In any case, it seems essential that opportunities for genuinely useful and constructive activities be available, so that offenders can be reinforced for applying themselves in socially desirable ways. In many cases, presently existing programs don't provide sufficient opportunities for reinforcement of alternative productive behaviors that actually will be useful in the world outside of the institution.

Skinner strongly advises that we look for good alternatives to punishment as ways of controlling behavior throughout society. He cautions that punishment is too often the easy way out. It often gives immediate results, and therefore we are deceived into believing that it is effective. At best, it is only a temporary answer, giving relief to the punisher as long as he or she is able to hold a threat of more punishment over the head of the violator. When the punisher or the threat is absent, the unwanted behavior is likely to recur, sometimes with a vengeance. The beaten child, the jailed criminal, the reprimanded employee, the severely disciplined student—there are many examples among such individuals of punished behavior that is repeated, sometimes in extreme fashion, when the chance arrives. According to Skinner, it is far better to find ways of applying positive reinforcement for "good" behaviors rather than waiting until "bad" behaviors occur and then relying on punishment. In his opinion, all social institutions should be structured so that persons systematically receive positive reinforcement for desirable behaviors. This would alleviate the need for the widespread use of punishment, because people would be conditioned to behave in individually and socially beneficial ways.

Considering three major concepts of Skinnerian psychology that have been discussed so far—reinforcement, punishment, and extinction—where do we stand in trying to explain human behavior? If we think of a person's life from birth to adulthood, we realize that the number and variety of behaviors emitted is tremendous. However, each person develops a unique set of behaviors that become common for him or her, and which in large part determine the individual's "personality." How do these particular behaviors get selected as the typical ways of responding, when so many other behavior patterns would have been possible? Skinner provides us with an answer. Some of the things we do are *reinforced* (either positively or negatively) and we continue them. Other behaviors have been *punished* and tend to be suppressed, at least under certain conditions. Still other behaviors have been *extinguished* and appear seldom or never. What gets reinforced, punished, or extinguished differs in various social settings. For example, aggressiveness may be reinforced in one society or family and punished in another. This helps to account for cultural and individual differences in behavior patterns.

Basically, this is the kind of broad analysis that Skinnerian psychology provides. In this form, the analysis is still somewhat crude and may not satisfy someone interested in understanding the finer points of human behavior. Some of the more subtle details need to be introduced, and this is the next objective.

GENERALIZATION
AND DISCRIMINATION

If *generalization* (or *induction*, as Skinner often calls it) didn't occur, we would have to learn each time how to respond in every new situation that we encounter. Obviously, we don't have to do this. We are able to deal with a variety of similar situations on the basis of our learning in particular situations. A person who learns how to drive one car also can drive other cars. A child who learns how to behave appropriately at the family dinner table also can behave properly at other dinner tables. Many situations have similar stimuli, and it is in the presence of these stimuli that we respond in ways that have been reinforced in the past. Generalization provides the advantage of "ready-made" responses in a variety of settings.

Skinner has used the following simple example to demonstrate generalization: If a pigeon is conditioned to peck a red spot, it will then also peck (at lower rates) an orange spot or a yellow spot, and spots with some variation in shape and size. (If the color were sufficiently different, for example green, then the pigeon would not be likely to peck.) A *generalization gradient* operates: responding tends to decrease in frequency as the stimuli become increasingly different from the initial stimulus (in this case, the red spot).

Despite its advantages, generalization isn't always a good thing. Though driving other cars is possible once one car has been mastered, transfer of similar responses may be disadvantageous if one car has an automatic transmission and the other has a manual transmission. Here is where *discrimination* saves the day, if this process occurs before an accident happens. We learn to distinguish different aspects of similar situations and our responses become more finely tuned to these subtle differences. This occurs when making similar responses is not reinforced. Trying to shift a manual transmission in the same way as an automatic won't work. Since that particular set of movements isn't reinforced, they eventually extinguish and are replaced by the appropriate manual transmission responses that are reinforced. In brief, then, discrimination refers to making different responses in various stimulus situations, and is basically the opposite side of the coin from generalization. Both processes are important in everyday life.

Skinner has demonstrated discrimination at a simple level by extending the pigeon example given above. As mentioned, once the bird has been conditioned to peck a red spot, the pecking generalizes to an orange spot. However, if reinforcement is changed so that it occurs *only* when the red spot is pecked, and never in the presence of orange, the pigeon eventually stops responding to the orange spot—discrimination has resulted. To give another example: If lever pressing by a rat is reinforced with food pellets when a light is on, but not when it's off, the lever eventually will be pressed only when the light is on.

In these examples, the red spot and the light have become *discriminative stimuli*. In their presence, responding has been reinforced. Discriminative stimuli exert considerable control over human behavior. Phones are answered only when they are ringing, strangers are approached more often when they are smiling than when they are frowning, and we drive through intersections only when the traffic light is green. The phone's ring, the stranger's smile, and the green light are discriminative stimuli— making the appropriate responses when these stimuli are present has been reinforced (someone usually has been on the line, strangers generally have been friendly, and we have moved through many intersections easily and safely).

The powerful influences that discriminative stimuli have on our lives is difficult to grasp unless some thought is given to it. Stop for a moment and think about how often your behavior is controlled by particular conditions that are present (often we are so predictably controlled that we call our behaviors "habits"). Skinnerian psychology maintains that the environment is a major determinant of our behavior and that we do not "choose" or "decide" to act in certain ways on the basis of some inner knowledge. Rather, the environment *selects* certain responses. Though we may feel that we are "freely deciding," for example, to approach a smiling stranger, Skinner maintains that both the decision and the approach are affected by the environmental conditions that we have experienced. In other words, the fact that approaching smiling strangers typically has been reinforced with returned friendliness is what determines *both* our decision and the approach behavior. It is not the decision that controls whether or not we will approach the person.

SHAPING

Most of the things we are able to do aren't learned by a one-shot process. Rather they are learned through the process of *shaping*. Eating with utensils, using tools properly, playing sports skillfully, reading, writing, and speaking a language, and many other abilities, develop in steps. Each bit of progress made toward the final behavioral goal is reinforced, but we have to keep moving toward that goal in order to keep the reinforcers coming. For example, very young children are praised for simply picking up a fork or spoon, but shortly they have to pick up food with it to gain their parents' attention. Next they have to hold it correctly, and finally they have to be able to get the food neatly into their mouths to receive approval. Step-by-step this process goes on, with reinforcement being given for progress and then being held back until more progress is shown.

Skinner suggests that language is learned in this way also. Utterances that vaguely resemble words are given attention and praise at first, and then progressively improving performance is required for further reinforcement. In this way, the child's verbal behavior is *shaped* until the language can be spoken in an acceptable way.

Endless examples of the shaping of constructive human behaviors could be given, but one more will suffice for now. Consider the skilled craftsman and the way in which his or her highly refined techniques develop. As an apprentice, small improvements in skill are reinforced, perhaps both by the comments of a master craftsman and the actual physical effect that the correct behaviors have on the materials being worked with. As time goes on, more and more improvements in technique have to be made in order to produce the desired effect and to earn the recognition of others, until finally the behaviors are very skilled.

Unfortunately, shaping also can have undesirable outcomes. For example, we may unknowingly shape annoying behaviors in others by ignoring (extinguishing) reasonable behaviors and reinforcing louder, more insistent actions with our attention. The parent who doesn't pay attention to the child's quiet requests, and then begins listening when the demands are intensified, may be paving the road toward loud, disturbing behavior. This kind of process happens in many different situations and is suggested by the common expression "the squeaky wheel gets the grease."

Violent, destructive behaviors can also be the result of shaping. For example, if a disadvantaged or oppressed group's reasonable demands are ignored by those in power, more intense demands are likely to result. These may bring some reinforcement in the form of concessions by the authorities. When this level of action no longer is attended to, the group may again escalate its efforts and thereby gain further advantages. If this step-by-step process continues, the end result may be violence, because that is what the group finally has to do to keep the attention of the authorities. This is similar to what happened in the 1960s as blacks and students escalated their methods of protest. Those in positions of authority would seem well advised to respond to moderate, reasonable requests for the correction of injustices, rather than waiting until they find themselves in the position of having to reinforce violent or disruptive actions.

As with other Skinnerian principles, shaping can be demonstrated in the relatively simple confines of a Skinner box. The lever-pressing rat and the key-pecking pigeon usually do not begin these behaviors suddenly. In other words, they don't simply go over and begin working on the lever or the key. They are led to these behaviors through shaping. For example, reinforcers (food pellets) may be given at first to the rat when it simply is at the end of the Skinner box where the lever is located. Then reinforcement is given only when the rat gets closer to the lever, and so on. When the animal is in the immediate vicinity of the lever (because that is where reinforcement has led it), it will sooner or later make a movement that involves touching the lever, and that response is then reinforced. Next, only responses that put pressure on the lever are reinforced, and so on, until actual pressing occurs and is reinforced a number of times.

By reinforcing behavior that is in the direction of the desired response (pressing the lever) and then withholding reinforcement until an even closer approximation of the desired response is made, the rat is led gradually toward lever pressing. After this operant-conditioning process has taken place, on later occasions the food-deprived animal will press the lever very soon after being placed into the Skinner box. A new operant behavior has been conditioned by using a shaping procedure.

In real life, shaping processes do not necessarily work smoothly to produce the best final behavioral products. Earlier, examples were given of children learning to use eating utensils and to speak a language, and of the process that leads to skilled craftsmanship. However, since many of our behaviors are shaped in unplanned and unsystematic ways by parents, teachers, peers, work supervisors, and others, the results frequently are less than desired. Several things can go wrong: (1) if a relatively crude response receives too much reinforcement, it may become so strong that more advanced responses do not occur—for example, parents may give so much attention to a child's early social behaviors that the child fails to develop more mature social responses (the child is "spoiled"); (2) if too rapid progress is attempted (the step to the next behavior required for reinforcement is too large), existing behavior may be extinguished before more advanced responses are emitted, thereby undoing the shaping that has taken place already—for example, a teacher may "expect too much" from a student and withhold approval for such a long time that the student's academic behaviors begin to decline rather than improve; (3) reinforcement for an advanced behavior may come too slowly, allowing other behaviors to occur in the meantime—the reinforcement may then strengthen these behaviors instead of the desired one (in other words, the wrong behaviors get reinforced)—for example, recognition that a worker gets long after completing an excellent job actually may reinforce poorer performances that have occurred in the meantime. Given the delicacy of the perfect shaping process, is it any wonder that we're so imperfect?

PROGRAMMED MATERIAL AND TEACHING MACHINES

Skinner has given considerable attention to the development of better techniques for shaping behavior. He suggests that many types of learning can be improved by the systematic application of

good shaping procedures, and he has been instrumental in planning the use of *programmed material* and *teaching machines.*
Constructing a "program" involves breaking down the subject
matter into small units. This ensures that the learner will be able
to make progress and not get stuck at a particular level because
the next step is too hard. In small sequential steps, the learner
moves toward better and better mastery of the material (mathematics, science, specific job-related information, or whatever).
Each effective step in learning the material is reinforcing.

There currently are many programmed textbooks that present material in small progressive steps. Also, various *teaching
machines* are in use. These devices present programmed material
in mechanically or electronically controlled ways. A unit of
material is displayed, the learner is required to make a response
that shows understanding of the material, and feedback is given
regarding the correctness of the response (if the program being
used is a good one, the learner almost always will respond
correctly). A teaching machine can provide the advantages of:
(1) keeping the learner busy—there are no long delays during
which the learner must sit and wait for more information;
(2) allowing the learner to move along at his or her own pace;
(3) complete mastery of each unit before the next one is presented; and (4) immediate reinforcement of correct responses by
letting the learner know he or she is correct. Skinner suggests that
there are strong similarities between teaching machines and the
private tutor who makes sure that the student understands the
material thoroughly, presents material for which the student is
prepared, and provides quick reinforcement for correct responses.
A good teaching machine and a good tutor are both effective
shapers of behavior.

In addition to these advantages, Skinner indicates that
teaching machines relieve teachers from the role of "drillmas-
ters," remove the need for aversive control (for example, students
do not have to be threatened with low grades), and reduce
needless competition among students. It is his belief that tremendous potential exists in the use of techniques based on

programmed instruction. One of the difficult problems is design-ing good programs, that is, breaking down various com-plex subjects into small, yet meaningful, units. This often is a tough job.

SCHEDULES OF REINFORCEMENT

Once a behavior has been shaped, it can be maintained by various patterns of reinforcement. Depending on the particular schedule, we may respond slowly or rapidly, show long pauses between responses, persistently respond despite the fact that we haven't been reinforced in a long time, and display other variations in behavior.

The two broad categories of schedules are *continuous* and *intermittent*. With the former, each response of a particular type is reinforced; in the Skinner box each time the rat presses the lever it gets a food pellet. With the latter, reinforcement occurs less than each time; for example, every fifth lever press is reinforced.

Regarding human behavior, the physical environment is much more likely to provide a schedule of continuous reinforce-ment than is the social environment. The outcomes of turning water faucets and pushing doors, and more complex behaviors such as bicycle riding, swimming, hitting a golf ball properly, or hand-weaving a rug, are all activities that deal with physical objects and have predictable outcomes. If these behaviors are performed in particular ways, reinforcement will occur each time. Although social situations are less likely to provide continuous reinforcement, there are exceptions. An acquaintance may always respond in a friendly way to your greetings, certain relatives might always be there when you need them, a certain person may always be fun to be with, and so on. Often, however, there is less consistency than this in our interactions with other people, and our social behaviors don't get reinforced every time.

Interestingly, when continuous reinforcement is interrupted, we often feel that something strange, disturbing, or perhaps humorous is going on. Skinner has used the example of the "house of mirrors" in an amusement park. The usual feedback is changed and we find it funny. Also, we may wonder or say something like "Isn't that odd?" if someone who has always been friendly suddenly ignores us. More seriously, we may experience severe "self-doubts" if we have been effective consistently in our efforts at school, on the job, or elsewhere, and suddenly some effort is not reinforced. In this situation, the person who is used to "ups and downs" (intermittent reinforcement) is not as apt to feel as discouraged as someone whose behavior has been reinforced continuously.

Extinction tends to occur relatively quickly if a behavior that has received continuous reinforcement is no longer reinforced. Assume that you are used to having a light come on every time you throw a switch. If it doesn't come on one day, you are more likely to give up sooner than if you are accustomed to a finicky switch that sometimes works and sometimes doesn't. In other words, continuous reinforcement leads to faster extinction than does intermittent reinforcement. This holds in social situations too. The person who has a long history of successes mixed with failures in forming friendships is apt to continue trying to relate to people even after a series of unsuccessful attempts. On the other hand, someone who always has made friends easily may give up if a few recent attempts have met with failure. One explanation for the differences in the behaviors of these two persons might emphasize inner qualities such as the greater "diligence" or "persistence" of the first individual. However, Skinner would say that the different reactions actually result from different schedules of reinforcement.

The fact that behaviors that have been maintained on a continuous schedule extinguish more rapidly than those on an intermittent schedule can be demonstrated vividly in the Skinner box. A pigeon may peck the key 50 to 100 times after reinforcement has been cut off, if it previously was on a schedule of continuous reinforcement. After some types of intermittent reinforcement, the bird will peck from 4000 to 10,000 times before extinguishing. Anyone who has tried to extinguish some human behavior after having reinforced it intermittently may have experienced these long-lasting effects. For example, parents who decide to extinguish their child's temper tantrums may find it frustrating and exhausting, especially if in the past they sometimes gave in to the child and sometimes resisted. For extinction purposes, at least theoretically, it would have been better if they had always given in, rather than just sometimes.

A few examples of human activities maintained by intermittent reinforcement are: writers who continue to produce even though their works are published infrequently; fishermen who go fishing time after time, but who catch fish only once every several times; gamblers who continue to play games of chance despite only occasional winnings; moviegoers who see film after film, but only once in awhile see a good one; and friends who continue seeing each other despite the fact that it isn't always reinforcing to be together. Lots of behaviors persist simply because they are reinforced occasionally.

Technically, there are two major types of schedules of intermittent reinforcement: *interval schedules* are based on passage of time and *ratio schedules* are based on number of responses. On an *interval schedule*, the first response made after an interval of time has passed is reinforced. Responses made before that go unreinforced. For example, you must wait an interval of time for water to boil before your response of pouring it on instant coffee will be reinforced. Also, checking your mailbox will not be reinforced with letters unless you wait an interval of time since the last mail delivery.

Intervals between reinforcement can be *fixed* or *variable*, and this is an important distinction. Our behavior will usually differ on these two types of interval schedules. On *fixed-interval* (FI) schedules, we tend to wait until the time when reinforcement will occur, and then begin our responses. If you always use the same pot, the same amount of water, and the same intensity of flame to boil the water, you have created a fixed-interval schedule. You probably will go calmly to the stove once, after the fixed interval has passed, and find water that's ready to be used. On the other hand, if you use different pots, different amounts of water, and turn the flame on carelessly, you will have a *variable-interval* (VI) schedule. Each time you boil water, you are likely to be running back and forth to the stove, checking the water.

Another good example of how FI and VI schedules can make us behave differently is this: Suppose that you are driven to work by a fellow employee who consistently arrives in front of your house at 7:30 A.M. (for our purposes this can be considered a fixed-interval schedule—the interval is exactly 24 hours long). Would your behavior differ from a situation in which your ride arrived sometimes at 7:30, sometimes at 7:39, other times at 7:21, and so on? Probably it would. On this variable-interval schedule, you would probably go to the window a number of times, checking to see if the person had arrived. Someone watching you would probably say that you were nervous, restless, or fidgety, but Skinner would say that your behavior was being affected by the variable-interval reinforcement schedule.

In the laboratory different results from fixed-interval versus variable-interval reinforcement schedules can be shown dramatically. For example, a pigeon on FI tends to pause after being reinforced, and then accelerates its pecking as the interval draws to an end and reinforcement again becomes available. On VI, the pigeon tends to maintain a constant rate of pecking, with little pausing. Skinner has given the example of birds on a VI schedule with an average interval of five minutes (the intervals varied around the five-minute mark, sometimes shorter, sometimes longer). They pecked for up to 15 hours, two or three times per second, with almost no pauses except to consume their reinforcers.

Ratio schedules yield reinforcers on the basis of number of responses made. Time is not a factor. These schedules also can be *fixed* (FR) or *variable* (VR). A rat working on FR might have to press the lever 20 times to get each food pellet, while on VR the number of presses would vary. For example, the *average* might be 20, but sometimes it would be 16, sometimes 24, and so on. Response patterns again differ on these two types of schedules. On

FR schedules, typically there are short pauses after reinforcement, followed by rapid responding. (With large ratios, there may be a significant period of slow responding after reinforcement. If the ratio is very large, there may be a long period of no response after reinforcement. Skinner has used the example of a student who finds it difficult to start work on the next assignment after finishing a term paper.) On VR schedules, the pauses are eliminated and responding is consistent. Generally, the response rates on *ratio* schedules are higher than on *interval* schedules.

The classic example of a *fixed-ratio schedule* at the human level is piecework: The worker gets paid a certain amount for each unit of work completed. Skinner says that this is a dangerous schedule because it can cause workers to push themselves to exhaustion. He suggests that it is too hard on salespersons, for example, to work solely on commission (which is a type of piecework). They should have some salary to supplement their commission, otherwise they may push themselves too much. The response pattern seen with animals in the Skinner box can also be seen among humans who are on strict FR schedules. They pause briefly after being reinforced (for example, after making a sale) and then work hard again until the next reinforcer.

Variable-ratio schedules also result in a high rate of activity, and pauses tend to disappear. Skinner has indicated that pigeons will peck for hours at a rate of five times per second on this type of schedule. An example frequently used by him to illustrate the dramatic effects that a VR schedule can have on human behavior is that of pathological gamblers. They make bet after bet, any of which might pay off. The outcome of any particular bet is unpredictable, but eventually they win (unfortunately, this occasional reward keeps the gambler going, even when the overall outcome is disastrous). Variable ratio schedules abound in our lives: calling our friends, watching TV, working hard at school or on the job, and a multitude of other behaviors, are not usually reinforced according to a fixed schedule. We may have successes two or three times in a row, then not get reinforced for the next several efforts, and so on.

The effects of schedules of reinforcement in our lives are not as neat and predictable as the effects seen in Skinner boxes. There are more complicating factors operating in real life. However, that doesn't negate the importance of such schedules in controlling our behaviors. It simply makes it much more difficult to specify exactly what is going on. We have only touched on the possible patterns of reinforcement that can operate. Skinner and a colleague, C. B. Ferster, published a book in 1957 titled *Schedules of Reinforcement*, in which they present the details of intermittent schedules on the basis of years of research. Two of the more complicated arrangements are *multiple schedules* (two or more schedules alternating randomly) and *concurrent schedules* (two or more independent schedules operating at the same time). There is much to consider regarding schedules of reinforcement. They make it clear that Skinnerian psychology can, at least theoretically, account for very complex human situations.

As a final example in this section, let's consider how different reinforcement schedules might affect sexual activity. Suppose that you are on a *variable-ratio schedule*. In other words, there is always the chance that the next approach to your lover will be reinforced with sexual activity. Isn't it likely that your approaches will be much more frequent and constant than if a pattern has been established by which your sexual advances are reinforced only after a week-long interval has passed? This latter schedule is a *fixed-interval schedule*, and would very likely result in long pauses followed by increased seductive approaches around the end of the week.

CHAINING

Chaining helps explain how we carry out smooth sequences of behavior. Sometimes it is difficult to understand how the reinforcement of specific responses can lead to activities such as playing the piano, walking to a restaurant through a maze of city streets, telling a long story, or going through the process of getting ready for school or work in the morning. In Skinner's view, these complex behavior patterns are made up of separate responses joined together in chains. Each response in a chain generates consequences that affect the next response. For example, a piano player's behavior is reinforced when he or she strikes the correct chord. Additionally, however, that chord provides the stimulus for the striking of the next chord, and so on, until the entire piece of music has been played.

The critical factor in chains of behavior is that *discriminative stimuli* can function as *conditioned reinforcers*. Discriminative stimuli indicate that a particular type of behavior, if emitted, is likely to be reinforced. Each response in a chain produces consequences that serve as discriminative stimuli for the next response, and which also reinforce the response just made. For example, walking into the kitchen puts one near the refrigerator; this may serve not only as the discriminative stimulus for opening its door but also may reinforce the response of "walking into the kitchen" (assuming that one is hungry). Each behavioral consequence in a chain can be analyzed in this way to show that it functions as *both* a discriminative stimulus and a conditioned reinforcer.

The final reinforcing event that maintains a chain of behavior may involve a primary reinforcer (for example, food). The food-deprived person gets *primary* reinforcement from eating and digesting food, but generally there are many responses that precede the actual act of eating. These responses are reinforced by conditioned reinforcers. Opening the refrigerator door is reinforced by the sight of food, reaching for the food is reinforced by holding the food, putting the food in the oven is reinforced by the smell of it cooking, and so on, until the food is finally eaten (primary reinforcement). The sight of food, the feel of food, and the smell of cooking are all conditioned reinforcers; each is also a discriminative stimulus for the response that follows it in the chain of behavior. They have acquired their reinforcing characteristics by being associated with the primary reinforcement derived from eating.

Typical non-Skinnerian explanations of sequences of behavior usually involve a lot of "decisions." To get something to eat, to go to bed, to visit a friend, to go to the movies, and so on, are commonly thought to involve conscious and deliberate choices.

Skinner's explanation removes the element of decision making or free choice, and focuses on the effects of stimuli and consequences on our behaviors.

Skinner and his colleagues have investigated the relationships between various environmental conditions and behavior. They have focused greatest attention on "contingencies of reinforcement"; this is a phrase often used by Skinner to refer to (1) behavior itself, (2) the conditions under which it occurs, and (3) its reinforcing consequences. Starting out with studies of rats and pigeons, they have formulated a number of basic behavioral concepts. Moving to the human level, many of their procedures have been applied effectively in a wide variety of situations with many different types of persons. Therefore, there now exists a substantial amount of evidence that Skinnerian psychology is applicable to human behavior.

In this chapter, many of Skinner's basic concepts were discussed. Some of the most important points were that (1) operant behavior can be strengthened through positive or negative reinforcement, (2) reinforcers can be either primary or conditioned, (3) some behaviors are "superstitious," that is, there is only an accidental connection between them and reinforcement, (4) operant behaviors that are not reinforced tend to extinguish, (5) punishment typically suppresses behavior but doesn't necessarily do so permanently, (6) responses that are reinforced in particular situations tend to generalize to similar situations, but discrimination develops if reinforcement occurs only in particular situations and not in others, (7) complex behaviors are shaped through the differential reinforcement of closer and closer approximations to the final behaviors, (8) different schedules of reinforcement yield different response rates, patterns of responding, and resistances to extinction, and (9) ongoing sequences of behavior can be considered as "chains" in which discriminative stimuli also serve as conditioned reinforcers.

FOUR

WHY IS
SKINNER
SO
CONTROVERSIAL?

Skinner has aroused more than his share of controversy. He may be the *most* controversial figure in the history of psychology, although Sigmund Freud, and perhaps John B. Watson (the founder of behaviorism) also merit consideration. Though the reasons why Skinner is so disputed are somewhat intertwined, they can be discussed separately:

1. Skinner's radical determinism contradicts the American ideal of self-determination. It opposes concepts of free choice, personal responsibility, and rugged individualism. Also, it follows that if our behavior is fully determined by past and present conditions, we can't "take credit for" our accomplishments.

2. He emphasizes that by controlling the environment we can control behavior and advocates that we should do this to improve our society and our lives. This disturbs those who don't like the connotations of the word "control" or the implications of "being controlled."

3. He originally based his suggestions for improving human behavior on findings from research with lower animals. There are critics who feel that such findings are not relevant to human activities and/or that it is insulting to apply them to humans.

4. His behavioral concepts have often been interpreted simplistically. This has resulted in criticism from those who feel that he either ignores or negates the richness of human life.

Each of these four sources of controversy will now be discussed in more detail.

THE AMERICAN IDEAL OF SELF-DETERMINATION VERSUS RADICAL DETERMINISM

Skinner isn't often taken lightly. He generally excites a definite reaction, sometimes positive, but often negative. He challenges certain established and cherished ways of thinking about ourselves, especially our emphasis on individual free choice and personal responsibility. Our economic, political, legal, and other social systems are based, in their ideal forms, on the view that each person is self-determining.

Skinner's approach conflicts with this view. He can be considered a radical determinist: an individual's *genetic inheritance, past history of personal experiences,* and *present environmental conditions* explain his or her behavior. Essentially, all three of these factors are environmental, because even genetic inheritance is determined by the influence of the environment on our evolutionary ancestors. This emphasis on environmental determinants of behavior refutes the American ideal of the strong, independent person who is self-determining, an individual who makes free choices and takes personal responsibility for "making something" of himself or herself.

Probably most of us would agree that *in fact* many aspects of our society do not operate according to individual free choice and responsibility, and that we often cannot really determine what our accomplishments will be. For example, our competitive economic system provides fair competition for only a minority. The rest do not have the means to compete effectively since they lack the necessary skills, material support, and/or appropriate opportunities. In the political realm, positions are held by those who supposedly have the "will and determination" to seek and win public office, but in reality it often seems that a background of money, prestige, and family influence are the determinants. Our legal system claims to administer justice fairly and makes the assumption that each individual is responsible (unless legally insane) for his or her own behavior. But would anyone argue that our legal institutions actually are equitable to rich and poor, white and black, powerful and powerless? Furthermore, most people would grant that not all persons, even when they are sane, are equally responsible for their criminal acts. Ignorance, extreme deprivation, and harshness of childhood experiences, as well as other factors, are often considered to be extenuating circumstances, even though the courts may not consistently take these factors into account.

The points to be made are these: The concept of individual responsibility and self-determination are well-ingrained in American society and continue to be held close to our hearts, despite the fact that our institutions (and many of our lives) are riddled with examples that deny freedom and equal opportunity for each person. Most of us have been taught that we are the masters of our own fates, at least to some degree. However, we've also learned that we must accept and live with certain disadvantages and that we shouldn't expect to get everything we want. In other words, "Yes, you are what you make of yourself through your own will power, personal fortitude, ingenuity, and so on," *but* (and this is the catch) "No, you will not necessarily have the same opportunities and advantages as others, and therefore you shouldn't expect to make out as well as you might like to." These two somewhat contradictory teachings suggest how we are able to maintain a vital belief in individual freedom of choice and determination, while the evidence around us reveals many limits and restrictions on what most of us accomplish.

Enter B. F. Skinner, who maintains that it is the environment (interpreted broadly to include all the social and physical conditions—past, present, and future—of which we are a part) that determines what we are and what we will become (remember, he accounts for genetic inheritance by referring to the environments that existed during evolutionary history). At first glance, this doesn't seem radical. The reaction might be: "Is he saying that we are affected by the environment? That makes sense. Obviously the conditions around us have some effect on us. I can accept that without any problem." As Skinner continues, however, it becomes clear that he is saying that environmental factors determine our behavior in such a way that "free will" and "individual choice" play no causal role.

The next reaction is apt to be a bit different from the first: "Now wait just a minute. Did I get that right? Our behavior is *completely* determined by conditions that have nothing to do with free thought or choice? That's ridiculous! I know some things are out of my control and that I don't get everything I want, but most of what I feel and do depends on *me*. If I don't feel like doing something, I don't do it. If I do decide to do something, I do it. *I* control things most of the time. Skinner goes way too far in what he's saying and I don't buy it."

It's the extent to which Skinner says we are influenced by the environment that causes controversy. He carries this assumption to a point where many people "don't buy it." As mentioned before, it violates what we have learned as members of a "free society" and goes against traditional concepts such as strong individualism, free choice, "being one's own person," and "making it" through personal drive and ingenuity. If your environment is primarily responsible for your success and determines your effectiveness, how can you be proud of your accomplishments? Where is the satisfaction if you don't do it on your own? These types of questions indicate the way people feel when they are asked to give up their ideas of self-determination. Though they are willing to agree that *sometimes* external factors and "luck" influence their fates, Skinner's more extreme position makes them feel that the very meaning of life is being challenged. Is it any wonder that Skinner stirs them up?

Most of us are willing to admit that we have had help in our achievements. Writers place acknowledgments at the front of their books, scientists thank colleagues and research-funding agencies, students express gratitude to their teachers, and athletes point out the debt they owe to their coaches. However, it is exceptional when a person relinquishes *all* credit for his or her good performance. More typically, we do take a large part of the credit ourselves (though to do so publicly in a blatant way is frowned on). Also, we usually expect to be admired for the "strong personal qualities" that bring us success.

The Skinnerian scheme of things doesn't allow for individual credit-taking in the usual sense. An individual is born with a given genetic makeup; certainly we deserve no credit for any unique hereditary qualities that we may have, since these qualities are bestowed in a way that is completely outside of our control. After birth, the social and physical environments exert their influences on us. Skinner suggests that these conditions also are not chosen or decided on by us, but rather are factors that simply exist and have effects. Therefore, we can take no greater credit for what we become after being born than we can for what we were at birth. In neither case do we freely choose or decide what conditions will affect us or what we will become.

This doesn't mean, though, that we aren't "individualistic," if that term can be changed somewhat from its usual meaning, which implies a kind of self-determined, freely chosen set of personal qualities. According to Skinner, each of us *is* unique (different from every other person) but not because we have chosen or decided to be so. Rather, our individualities spring from two facts: Our genetic structures differ (except in the case of identical twins) *and* each of us is exposed to somewhat different experiences. It would be impossible for two persons (even identical twins) to have precisely the same experiences in every detail. These variations contribute to producing individuals who differ from one another. An important point here is that dramatic differences in experiences are not necessary to produce different "personalities." Even subtle, perhaps almost unnoticeable, differences can have an effect.

It isn't hard to accept this type of reasoning, to a point. The idea that hereditary factors and early life experiences are outside of individual control seems very reasonable. But, once again, Skinner carries things beyond what is reasonable to many people by suggesting that the influence of environmental factors does not diminish as we grow older. He does suggest that we may become increasingly able to deal effectively with our environmental conditions because of our expanding behavior repertoires. In other words, with maturity we usually are capable of making a greater variety of responses, especially if a variety of constructive and adaptive behaviors have been reinforced, and this gives us a certain amount of "independence." It is not an independence based on free choice and autonomy, however. Rather, it is based on the increased quantity and types of responses we can make, and this depends on our physiological development and learning experiences.

For Skinner, there is no developing ego or self that eventually is able to take over and give deliberate, conscious, rational direction to our lives. In other words, the individual is not able, even with maturity, to wrestle control away from external factors and become removed from environmental control. We remain, in Skinner's eyes, under the influence of our environments from birth to death. This is a foreign and aggravating opinion to many people. Who wants to believe that he or she can't rise above surrounding circumstances and be free and autonomous? This is a cherished hope and belief that Skinnerian psychology tampers with, and those who hold it get impatient, annoyed, or angry when it is challenged.

THE CONCEPT OF CONTROL

Tied closely to the strict determinism of Skinner's approach is his repeated use of the term "control." This is another major cause of the controversy that churns around Skinner. Control is important in Skinnerian psychology in various ways, but the basic assumption is that environmental conditions control (that is, either maintain or change) behavior in systematic ways. This assumption goes back to Skinner's early work with animals in the laboratories at Harvard University and has remained with him through his many years as a researcher, teacher, lecturer, and writer. It is a concept with much supporting evidence. The laboratory studies of Skinner and others have shown time and again that if conditions are set in certain, specified ways, the behavior of rats, pigeons, and other lower animals can be predicted with a great deal of precision. For example, if a hungry rat receives a food pellet (a reinforcer) whenever it presses the lever in a Skinner box, it will soon press the lever repeatedly whenever it has been deprived of food. Also, the rate at which the rat works can be changed by altering the number of presses required to receive reinforcers. These are very simple examples. Laboratory studies have revealed many more complex relationships between environmental manipulations and behavioral outcomes. Also, it is very important to realize that research on environmental effects is not limited to animal studies. Humans have been studied under various environmental conditions, and it has been shown that we too are susceptible to their influence and often respond predictably.

The concept of control, then, became central in Skinner's thinking at an early stage of his work as a psychologist. Though at first concentrating on the ways in which he could set conditions in order to get reliable, predictable behaviors from lower animals, he eventually extended his findings to include the control of human behavior. According to Skinner, humans also are subject to the controlling influences of environmental factors and therefore social conditions can be set up in ways that will yield predictable behavioral outcomes. Frequently he has suggested that we should take seriously the idea of cultural design and plan our social institutions so that people will be productive, secure, creative, healthy, and happy. He feels that too often these things are left to chance rather than being planned.

As in the case of radical determinism, discussed previously, a moderate version of Skinner's suggestions would arouse little disagreement. Who would deny that we should look carefully at our society and try to make it better through constructive changes? It is the extreme nature of the proposal that provokes people and this extremism becomes embodied in the word CONTROL. Using the term repeatedly, Skinner does more than simply consider desirable changes in social conditions and institutions: He advocates that we accept the unalterable fact that we *are* controlled and that we then move ahead and plan the environment in such a way that society runs smoothly and beneficially. Few of us want to be convinced that we actually are controlled by forces outside of ourselves, but Skinner continually rubs our faces in that assumption. "Freedom" is what most persons want to hear about, not "control."

Additional aspects of the control issue also get people upset. *Who* is to do the controlling and *to what ends?* Skinner himself is not always clear in his responses to these questions but has indicated that persons already in positions to exert control could be more effective if they knew and used his psychological concepts. These persons are parents, teachers, supervisors, and others in charge of making or implementing decisions. However, a common fear among Skinner's critics is that the power to control will become invested in some dictatorial group, who will then apply behavior-control procedures for their own ends. Sometimes Skinner is accused of providing information that can be abused by power-hungry individuals.

Another question is: How could we decide which behaviors to control? Skinner has suggested that we could agree on certain desirable goals, such as happiness, productivity, and creativity. We could then go ahead and systematically experiment with techniques for controlling the environmental conditions that produce these outcomes. Though this seems like a simple proposal, it isn't always seen in that light. Skinner has been criticized for being too general and vague. Wouldn't there be conflict about the specifics of happiness, productivity, creativity, etc.?

GENERALIZATIONS
FROM ANIMALS TO HUMANS

The origin of Skinner's concepts of behavior control—laboratory studies of rats and pigeons—is another point that makes his ideas controversial. Even though there have been numerous successful applications of Skinnerian concepts at the human level, their original source is not forgotten and continues to be criticized and resented. Criticism often centers around the idea that the complexity of humans puts them into an entirely different category from lower animals and therefore any observed similarities in behavior are more apparent than real. The argument is made that even though certain common relationships may be observed between environmental manipulations and behavioral outcomes in both animals and humans, the dynamics differ. For example, the behaviors of both rats and humans tend to increase in frequency when certain consequences occur, but is the reason the same? Perhaps humans "figure out" what is going on by using rational thought processes and then "decide" to behave as they do in order to get reinforced. With rats the process may be more "mechanical," that is, determined by the neurophysiological makeup of the organism with no conscious or rational self-determination taking place.

There also are those who just plain resent likening humans to animals. They feel that to listen to ideas that grew out of animal research is to degrade the human condition. They don't want to deal with a psychology that had such lowly beginnings and feel that behavioral concepts and procedures drawn from studies of rats and pigeons are unfit for humankind. They are offended by Skinner's attempts to look at our behavior in a light similar to that in which he observed his laboratory animals.

SIMPLE BEHAVIORAL ANALYSIS

Still another aspect of Skinnerian psychology arouses controversy: its apparent simplicity, which sometimes is translated as "oversimplification." The following comments are typical: "Maybe what Skinner is saying is correct as far as it goes, but it certainly doesn't apply to the full complexity of human behavior. His system is absurdly oversimplified. He doesn't even begin to capture the richness of human life." The assumption frequently made is that Skinner doesn't deal with human feelings and thoughts and that he has nothing to say about complex behaviors such as those displayed in creative activities. Even persons who know that he does discuss these matters often are not satisfied with his explanations. In either case, whether it is believed that Skinner avoids such issues or that his formulations are inadequate, there is cause for strong reactions. He has been accused of pushing a system that ignores the full meaning of being human.

In the next chapter, the sources of controversy indicated here are discussed again, for the purpose of pointing out misunderstandings that sometimes intensify the criticisms that are made of Skinner's approach. In addition, several other topics that are especially likely to cause misunderstandings are covered.

FIVE

WHAT ARE SOME OF THE COMMON MISUNDERSTANDINGS ABOUT SKINNER?

At least in part, the controversy that Skinner generates is due to misunderstandings of what he is saying. The reasons for these misunderstandings involve both Skinner and his audience. Some of his writings are difficult to grasp in detail. On the other hand, not all of Skinner's critics read his works with sufficient care.

In chapter 4, four major reasons were given for the controversy over Skinner's ideas. Those reasons gain even more power to arouse disputes if misunderstandings exist. Let's look briefly at each of them again to try to clarify Skinner's actual positions. The goal is not to explain away all sources of controversy, but rather to clear away confusion and possible misinterpretations. There will continue to be those who have real disagreements with Skinner; opposition based on a thorough understanding of what he has said can be stimulating and productive.

SELF-DETERMINATION
VERSUS
RADICAL DETERMINISM

It is quite true that Skinner denies that our behaviors are self-determined by our inner states of mind or emotion. Rather, he explains behavior by pointing to genetic inheritance and (most importantly) individual experiences with surrounding social and physical environments. In his view, then, we are not self-determining in the usual sense of that phrase. Also, certain traditional American ideals, such as personal responsibility and rugged individualism, have little place in his scheme of things. Skinner believes that our devotion to such ideals has hindered progress toward developing a society in which citizens are more productive, creative, secure, and happy. He suggests that we rely too heavily on assumed inner qualities (personal motivation, drive, will power, fortitude, and so on) for the determination of success. We talk about freedom and opportunity for all, hoping to encourage individual efforts and achievements, but, in Skinner's opinion, this is a relatively ineffective way to improve life and to ensure the continued survival of a strong society. It leaves too much to chance. Too many persons get passed by and spend their lives in apathy or frustration, not being able to develop their potential, missing opportunities to improve themselves, and failing to contribute to society.

Skinner believes that it would be far more effective to use available information about the effects of environmental factors on behavior, information that has come from studies of both animals and humans. He suggests that by doing this (that is, by engaging in behavioral engineering) environments can be developed that will benefit both individuals and society. In brief, Skinner advocates that we give up our reverence for self-determination, face the facts, and turn toward environmental planning, since it is the environment that can be counted on to influence behavior.

A major misunderstanding regarding these issues is the common belief that Skinner's proposals are totally (or almost totally) opposed to our most cherished ideals. Though he does challenge self-determination by denying that we freely and autonomously decide or choose how we are going to behave, he strongly supports other important traditional beliefs: the ideals of maximizing each person's potential, creating more happiness and satisfaction, and having a strong and effective society. He wants his principles to be used to accomplish these goals.

Another misunderstanding sometimes arises out of Skinner's attack on the concept of personal responsibility (which is related closely to self-determination). He reasons that since we all are products of genetic and environmental factors, it isn't reasonable to hold individuals responsible for their behaviors. This worries those who feel that widespread acceptance of Skinner's ideas would bring on a rash of irresponsible and criminal behaviors by people who would say: "I'm not responsible for what I do. Circumstances are at fault. Don't blame me." Two points need to be made here. First, this type of excuse already is used by many delinquents, criminals, and others who behave in antisocial ways. Skinner provides no new excuse for them. Second, our present system of placing personal responsibility on people is not notably successful. We have plenty of irresponsible and criminal behavior in our society. Maybe such behaviors could be reduced by relying less on individual responsibility and more on the careful analysis and restructuring of environmental conditions.

Skinner points out that maximum study and use of constructive environmental changes is delayed by clinging to the notion of personal responsibility (and this is his main reason for objecting to it). Of course, we already accept to some extent the fact that environmental factors affect behavior, and various social programs are designed to reduce delinquent, criminal, and other undesirable activities. However, by Skinner's standards these often are half-hearted attempts based on faulty behavioral concepts or procedures. According to him, a more consistent, rigorous, and informed effort is needed.

There also is misunderstanding regarding the phrase "self-determination." Actually, the phrase can be used in Skinnerian psychology if its meaning is altered somewhat. In fact, as will be discussed later in this chapter, Skinner sometimes uses a closely related phrase: "self-control." As noted repeatedly, Skinner's ideas are opposed to traditional connotations of "self-determination." But, in a different sense, people *do* influence their environments, which, in turn, influence them. In other words, we aren't simply passive organisms. Almost all of Skinner's behavioral concepts are based on the fact that we are active and responsive. As we behave, we affect the social and physical worlds around us; we alter our environments. These alterations then affect us. There is an interaction between us and our environments. *Ultimately, it is the en-*

vironment that has control, but our behaviors (because they act to change the environment) play a role in the types of influence that the environment has. This issue will be discussed in more detail shortly.

As mentioned previously, in Skinner's radical determinism no room is given to an ego, a self, or any other inner autonomous agent that might direct our behavior. He rejects the idea that such internal agents allow us to make independent and free choices. Accordingly, our choices and decisions are never really free. They always depend on our basic genetic structure and, very importantly, our exposure to a multitude of environmental conditions. We can never be free from these influences; they are always the final determinants of our behavior.

This has been criticized as an unacceptable, or even ridiculous, philosophy. If Skinner were correct, wouldn't it be completely depressing to live out one's life? Wouldn't everything be so predictable that the anticipation and excitement of life would be gone? Again we are moving into an area where misunderstandings are likely to occur. As Skinner has suggested, to say that we live completely *determined* lives doesn't lead to the conclusion that we live completely *predictable* lives. In the first place, it is impossible to be absolutely certain about all of the genetic characteristics of a person. Though these genetic characteristics exist and influence behavior, they are not completely knowable to the person or to others. In other words, neither we nor others can be certain what the effects of our genes will be.

The same can be said about the environment. Even when a great deal is known about one's environment, it isn't possible to know everything. Subtle environmental factors can affect behavior, so it isn't possible (with presently existing techniques) to make *completely* accurate predictions about behavioral outcomes. Also, various unique interactions between genetic and environmental factors can occur, causing other unpredictable outcomes. Taking all these considerations into account, one can agree with Skinner's radical determinism and still look forward to a life that is unpredictable and exciting.

There might appear to be a contradiction here of earlier statements about the possibilities of using behavioral engineering. Skinner advocates the planning of environmental conditions so that behaviors beneficial to individuals and to society will be developed and maintained. But can this occur if behavior is as unpredictable as has just been suggested? The answer to this is that predictability isn't an all-or-nothing affair. By carefully controlling certain environmental conditions, the likelihood of getting certain desired behavioral outcomes is increased significantly. However, some unpredictability always will exist, even in a society carefully controlled along Skinnerian lines. It is likely that certain genetic and environmental factors, and their effects on behavior, will continue to remain unknown. This doesn't invalidate Skinner's deterministic view; it simply means that some of the multitude of factors that affect our behaviors will remain uncontrolled and therefore some behaviors will not be completely predictable.

Yet another misunderstanding that derives from Skinner's strict determinism is the implication that we are *completely* at the whim of either fate or the controlling influences of others. Critics have pointed to the fatalism that they feel is inherent in his philosophy. How can anything have any meaning in a system based on such an assumption? Aren't we simply pawns in a game if radical determinism is true? In response to such questions, it must be pointed out that according to Skinner each of us does have an effect on the social and physical environments with which we have contact. They are altered by each of us. The individual counts, in the sense that each person's behaviors are a real part of the real world, and therefore influence that world.

Though these statements might appear to indicate some backsliding from the position of strict determinism, they are not really inconsistent with Skinner's view. Because of genetic endowment, past experiences, and present circumstances, we *will* behave in certain ways (in other words, our behavior *is* determined). The behaviors that we emit, however, change the environment in some way, that is, produce consequences of some sort. These consequences in turn affect our behaviors, and so on. According to Skinner, each of us is a vital link, *a unique locus of events*, in this process. Therefore our behaviors *are* meaningful in that they produce environmental changes that affect us. To refer back to an earlier point, though we are not self-determining in the traditional sense of having free choice about how we behave, we can be considered self-determining in the Skinnerian sense that our actions have outcomes that influence our future behaviors. We are not simply pawns in a game, since the behavior of each individual, based on his or her own particular hereditary and experiential factors, is unique.

This gets us back to the important issue of credit-taking, discussed in chapter 4. Does the reasoning in the previous paragraph mean that we can take some personal credit for our accomplishments, since these accomplishments are unique and individualistic contributions? However comforting it might be to answer "Yes" to this question, in the strict Skinnerian sense the answer is "No." Each of us does make unique and individualistic contributions, but not because of some special inner quality. Rather, these contributions derive from each person's special genetic structure, special experiences, and special circumstances—and none of these conditions is something for which the person can take credit. We do not, through admirable acts of free and autonomous judgment or choice, determine these factors.

THE CONCEPT OF CONTROL

One of the most frequent misunderstandings of Skinner's emphasis on control is the assumption that it's a one-way process. The mere mention of controlling environmental factors in order to control human behavior disturbs persons who think in terms of free and independent action. When it is believed additionally that control works solely in a hierarchical fashion, from controller to controllee, it is even more upsetting (perhaps it stirs up ideas of dictatorial control).

However, in situations designed according to Skinner's suggestions, the controller-controllee distinction is minimized; there is no concentration of power in the controller. Let's assume that the controller is a person appointed or selected to establish goals and/or regulate behavior. Though this is a position of influence, Skinner reminds us that (in a well-planned system) those being managed by the controller also have a good deal of power to *countercontrol* (that is, they can directly and significantly influence the controller). This countercontrol ensures against the misuse of power by controllers.

Countercontrol can take various forms. Ideally, both controllers and controllees are reinforced for their appropriate behaviors. In a Skinnerian society, the controllers (for example, teachers, parents, and supervisors) attempt to control the environment in such a way that clearly stated behavioral outcomes result. In order to get these behavioral outcomes, Skinner suggests that the best methods are those based on the use of positive reinforcement. Some positive reinforcers are material things such as money and food. Other positive reinforcers are more socially based: praise, attention, and so on. Another type of positive reinforcer is simply "being effective." Skinner points out that this seems to be a very basic feature of humans: Often our behaviors are reinforced simply by the environmental changes they produce, rather than by some material or social reinforcer.

Clearly, then, controllers have a variety of positive reinforcers with which to control behavior. But how about the controllees? What can they use to countercontrol? Perhaps the most direct means is their performance. If the controllers are doing their jobs properly, the controllees will perform well. Good performance reinforces the controller because it shows that he or she has been effective. (Being effective, of course, may lead to other reinforcers for the controller: pay raises, promotions, praise from others, etc.) On the other hand, poor performance on the part of controllees is likely to be punishing to the controller, and may cause him or her to revise those methods which are causing poor performance.

If the situation deteriorates, for example, if the controller moves to aversive methods such as threats of punishment for poor performance, then other countercontrolling measures may be used by controllees. They may leave the situation (for example, the student may cut classes, the child may run away from home, and the employee may fake illness or quit the job); they may aggress against the controller (for example, talking back to a teacher, parent, or supervisor); they may produce other aversive conditions for the controller (the student may "act up" and disrupt the class, the child may throw temper tantrums, and the employee may use sabotage). Obviously these methods of countercontrol do not allow a smooth-running, effective, and pleasant situation. Therefore, as Skinner repeatedly emphasizes, it is important to plan situations so that positive reinforcement is distributed without the necessity of *aversive* controlling and counter-controlling measures. It is interesting to ask: "How many controller-controllee situations in our present society are characterized by mutual reinforcement in the absence of aversive conditions?"

Getting back to the main point that launched us into this discussion of methods of countercontrol, it must be emphasized again that countercontrol is a vital part of Skinner's plan. If this is remembered, it helps offset the possible misinterpretation that those being controlled in a Skinnerian society would be powerless victims of manipulations by controllers. Skinner is well aware of the dangers inherent in situations in which people lack the power to countercontrol effectively. In fact, he points out that it is instructive to look at five groups of people in our present society who have little countercontrolling influence: the aged, young children, retarded persons, prisoners, and psychotics. They are frequently treated poorly, with a lack of compassion. They generally don't have the means to exert effective countercontrol, and therefore have to rely on the intervention of others on their behalf. In a society using Skinner's behavioral principles, safeguards would be set up to ensure better treatment of these persons. In other words, "compassion" would be ensured through environmental control.

As stated before, the connotations of the word "control" get

Skinner into a lot of trouble. It seems opposed to the dignity of human life. But is this a valid assumption or is it a misunderstanding of what Skinner is saying? What Skinner typically means when he recommends "control," is that environmental conditions be altered in order to establish desirable behaviors. The "undignified" aspect of this goes back to issues that were discussed earlier; it challenges traditional assumptions about humans as free, autonomous, and self-determining. However, if better environmental control resulted in more productive, happy, healthy, and creative people, wouldn't that *increase* our dignity or worth? This partly depends on what is valued most: holding onto traditional concepts of human dignity and freedom, *or* attempting to control the environment to improve our behaviors.

One final comment will be made about control, in response to two questions that often are asked: "If Skinner's concepts of control are valid, isn't there a danger that they'll be used by malevolent persons to benefit themselves? Isn't Skinner suggesting the means by which such persons can control others for selfish reasons?" As Skinner himself has admitted, his behavioral concepts and procedures can be misused. There is no absolute, foolproof way of guarding against this possibility, but the same is true of many other types of knowledge. (Skinner has used the example of atomic energy, which can be used for good or evil purposes.) However, there are quicker and easier ways for evil persons to get their way; they can and do use threats, physical force, and other aversive methods. Skinner's proposals for controlling behavior advocate the systematic use of positive reinforcement, rather than aversive methods of control.

GENERALIZATIONS FROM ANIMALS TO HUMANS

There is no doubt that Skinner's early attempts to discuss human situations and problems, and his suggestions for improvements, were based heavily on findings from his laboratory studies using rats and pigeons as subjects. For example, his novel, *Walden Two*, written in 1945, was an attempt to apply what he had learned about behavioral control to the construction of a utopian community. He believed that behavioral concepts developed by studying lower animals in carefully designed and controlled experiments might apply at the human level.

Since the publication of *Walden Two*, much additional research has been carried out, using both animal and human subjects. Studies have been done with psychotic, neurotic, retarded, and normal children and adults. Skinner's ideas and procedures have been used effectively by psychologists and others in settings such as schools for delinquents, hospitals and institutions, public schools, colleges and universities, therapists' offices, and family situations. Under various circumstances, delinquent behaviors have been changed; psychotics and retardates have been trained to be more self-sufficient; behavioral and learning problems among school children have been reduced; students have learned more efficiently using teaching machines and programmed instruction; therapists have helped clients change their troublesome and maladaptive behaviors; and parents have been instructed in the use of behavioral procedures for interacting more effectively with their children. The list of places where Skinnerian practices have been applied at the human level could go on, and would include businesses, nursing homes, day-care centers, and rehabilitation wards.[1]

Considerable evidence now exists that Skinner's behavioral techniques (often referred to as "operant procedures") are effective with humans in a wide variety of situations. No longer can his psychology be considered as primarily applying to rats and pigeons; it has gone far beyond its origins. The phrase "behavior modification" has become common, referring to the application of Skinnerian methods (as well as certain behavioral principles developed by others) to human problems and situations.

[1] For a popular article on the spreading use of behavior modification, see Kenneth Goodall, "Shapers at Work," *Psychology Today*, November 1972, pp. 53–63, 132–138. Also, see Alan E. Kazdin, "The Rich Rewards of REWARDS," *Psychology Today*, November 1976, pp. 98–105, 114.

The criticism that Skinner overgeneralizes from simple animal studies to complex human behaviors has never been a very sound one. He has never said that humans and lower animals are just alike, but rather has drawn *assumptions* about human behavior from animal research. The mistake would be to say: "We know this about rats and pigeons; therefore we also know this about humans." Skinner's approach has been to use findings from animal research to formulate behavioral concepts that can be tested out at the human level. In other words, once it has been found that certain environmental events or conditions are related to certain behavior patterns among rats or pigeons, the question is: "Do similar relationships between environmental factors and behavior exist for humans?" Findings from animal studies may *possibly* hold true at the human level. However, it is always a matter of collecting data to verify that they do. In the case of *Walden Two*, it must be remembered that it is a novel and was not written as an *actual* account of the application of Skinner's concepts at the social level. It was an account of the *possibilities* of applying his concepts. As Skinner has stated, he was "guessing" when he wrote the book. If written today, because of the widespread use of behavior-modification programs, less guessing would be required.

Though there is little real basis for faulting Skinner on the issue of generalizing from lower animals to humans, there is another criticism concerning overgeneralization that carries more weight. There is a difference between using behavioral procedures effectively in carefully circumscribed settings within mental institutions, school systems, business organizations, and so on, and their application at the larger level of society as a whole. In his 1971 book, *Beyond Freedom and Dignity*, and in other publications as well, Skinner makes bold proposals for changes in our social system, strongly suggesting that the very survival of our society may depend on the adoption of a behavioral-engineering approach. He doesn't say simply that behavior modification has been used successfully in a wide variety of human situations and that its use should therefore be extended; he goes well beyond that, recommending, in essence, that the social structure be revamped along Skinnerian lines.

This proposal has caused heated reactions. Is Skinner justified in making society-wide claims for his approach on the basis of its past and current effectiveness? As indicated, the successes are numerous. Still, these successes derive mainly from behavior-modification programs carried out in situations, and under circumstances, that are quite specific and limited when compared with the extent and complexity of major political, legal, economic, and other social institutions. It is debatable, despite the evidence that has accumulated since the 1950s, that Skinner's behavioral techniques would be effective if applied on a massive scale. Also, too little is known about the possible dangers and drawbacks of society-wide application. Perhaps he is being premature in advocating total acceptance of his approach.

In fairness to Skinner, it must be pointed out again that embedded in his behavioral-engineering approach is a safeguard that should help prevent any serious damage to society's fabric from the adoption of his ideas. This safeguard essentially is the experimental method: If a condition is altered, its effects are observed carefully. By observing relationships between environmental manipulations and behavioral outcomes, progress can be monitored and changes can be made if necessary. If this approach is used, the chances of getting way off the track are lessened considerably. Of course, there still are opportunities for human errors such as poor data collection and biased conclusions, but these are present under any system and perhaps are less likely to occur with a behavioral-engineering approach because of its continual emphasis on the need for careful observations. Skinner also has suggested that we should think about forming small experimental communities (like Walden Two) in order to test out various behavioral approaches. On a small scale, it would be easier to implement changes and to observe their effects.

Before going to the next section, a final point will be made. As mentioned in chapter 4, some critics have said that even though lower animals and humans sometimes obey similar behavioral principles, they do so for different reasons. Rats and pigeons may behave "automatically," without thinking, but humans think and make decisions. For example, if a rat presses a lever again after having received a food pellet for the previous press, this may be simply a mechanical-type response, involving no higher thought processes. However, if a person repeats a response that has just been reinforced, he or she may have "figured out" what's going on and "decided" to behave in the way that will bring reward. This line of reasoning sometimes is used against Skinner's assumption that humans are influenced by environmental events in ways similar to animals.

In reply, it must be admitted that it is very hard to disprove the idea that conscious decisions lie behind most human behaviors. However, if time and again it can be shown that particular environmental events have predictable behavioral outcomes, is there any good reason to assume that human behavior is guided by thought? Thinking may be going on, but is it this thinking *or* the environmental event that determines the behavior. Two things (thought *and* some event) are occurring. Which is the actual cause of the behavior? Skinner votes for the environmental event and says that the accompanying thought processes are not influential. In fact, they too are influenced by what is occurring environmentally. (This issue will be taken up again soon, in the section "Feelings and Thoughts.")

SIMPLE BEHAVIORAL ANALYSIS

Is Skinner's analysis of human behavior really oversimplified? Certainly there are many critics who claim it is. Again, misunderstandings sometimes are at the root of these claims. One of the popular conceptions (or misconceptions) of Skinnerian psychology is that it simply states the obvious: Behaviors can be strengthened by their consequences. One such consequence is *positive reinforcement*, the backbone of Skinner's approach. It may seem to be simple folk wisdom, meaning that we all are likely to do what pays off in money, prestige, attention from others, sexual contacts, or other "rewards" for our efforts. After all, don't sales-persons sell to earn commissions, students study for good grades, children "act up" to get the attention of their playmates, and lovers behave romantically to have sexual relations? So what's the big deal about "positive reinforcement?" Why is it anything special? Isn't it just a simple idea, one that we all know works in certain situations?

The apparent simplicity of positive reinforcement is deceptive. Skinner and his colleagues have used it to get animals and humans to perform very complex behaviors. A good example at the human level is "programmed instruction." By reinforcing very simple correct responses at first, then requiring more and more advanced responses for reinforcement, the student is led, stepwise, toward the development of complex skills and knowledge. (For adults, simply being informed that they have given the correct answer usually is sufficient reinforcement to keep them working.) Of course, this is what is supposed to occur in most training programs and classrooms. But, as Skinner points out, this process often occurs in a relatively inefficient manner; typically the material to be learned is not broken down into sufficiently small units (thereby causing confusion) and the student's behavior is not reinforced in a systematic way. It is important, for example, to provide immediate reinforcement; the student should be given immediate feedback about the correctness of his or her answers. In contrast, students in the typical classroom often do not receive examination results until quite some time has passed.

Skinner maintains that much learning, in both classrooms and the outside world, is controlled by positive reinforcement, but the efficiency and degree of learning could be improved greatly by attention to how and when reinforcers are administered. In other words, Skinner's so-called "simple" concept, positive reinforcement, has widespread applications throughout society. Even if the concept itself seems simple, the many behaviors that are affected by it include those that are very complex. If only the end products are seen (for example, the ability to operate complicated machinery and equipment, to solve mathematical problems, to play sports skillfully, or to use involved scientific methods), it is difficult to imagine how Skinner's analysis could be relevant. However, what must be remembered is that these abilities are not learned all at once. They are learned step-by-step, sometimes efficiently, sometimes inefficiently.

According to Skinner, appropriately applied positive reinforcement (for example, immediate positive feedback about the correctness of one's behavior) can foster enjoyable, rapid, and thorough learning. On the other hand, lack of appropriate, systematic reinforcement can make learning unpleasant, slow, and careless. (In many cases, "rules" also promote learning; for example, a person may receive verbal instructions regarding the operation of a machine or the application of a scientific procedure. Skinner refers to "rule-governed" behavior to indicate that it isn't always necessary for us to be exposed to actual circumstances in order to learn. Of course, rule-following behavior itself is affected by reinforcement: If following the instructions, advice, warnings, etc. of others is reinforced, such behavior is strengthened. More will be said about this shortly.)

To refer back to an earlier paragraph, it's true that we all know that the salesperson's commissions, the student's grades, the attention a child gets, and so on, can influence their behaviors. But simply to acknowledge these influences on behavior does not show that we understand all that Skinner means when he discusses positive reinforcement. There are multitudes of positive reinforcers that operate in peoples' lives, some very obvious (like money, report cards, and orgasms) and others more subtle (like nods of approval, gentle touches, and casual complimentary remarks). Also, the consequences of behaviors such as turning doorknobs, reaching for objects, or moving one's head to increase visibility, can be reinforcing. All of these can affect behavior. To Skinner the details of how, when, and where reinforcers are received go a long way toward explaining human behavior in its simple and complex forms, at work, school, home, and else-where. In these details lie the factors that make the Skinnerian concept of positive reinforcement more than an obvious over-simplified version of common knowledge.

A few final comments can be made about simplicity and Skinner's system of psychology. First, as indicated in chapter 3, there are a number of concepts beyond positive reinforcement that Skinner uses to explain behavior: negative reinforcement, punishment, extinction, generalization, discrimination, and so on.

Second, the complexity of operant-conditioning research has reached the stage where Skinner himself has admitted that he doesn't understand some of it. Current work on the relationships among situational factors, behaviors, and consequences is being done by many behaviorally oriented researchers, some of whom are using computers in their laboratories (for example, to provide intricate patterns of reinforcement). The published studies of such research often are so technical that they can be understood only by a small group of specialists.

Third, Skinner's concept of "rule-governed" behavior makes it clear that our actions can be influenced by advice, suggestions, instructions, and other verbal stimuli, thereby including in his psychology many complex behaviors that are sometimes mistak-enly thought to be outside its realm. In his view, behavior often is determined by its consequences, but the consequences need not actually be experienced directly. Being told what they will be can also be effective. Though much of our behavior is "contingency-shaped" (shaped by direct, natural consequences), the following of "rules" also is common. For example, as Skinner has indicated, learning to drive a car involves both rule-governed and contin-gency-shaped behaviors. The learner is given verbal directions to supplement the consequences that occur from behaviors such as depressing the clutch, moving the shift lever, pressing the accel-erator, turning the steering wheel, etc. (It's important to re-member that rules themselves come about because of consequences that have occurred; they then describe, state, or imply behaviors and consequences to those who have not been exposed to the original situations. If it were not for rule-governed behavior, each individual's behaviors would be influenced only by natural consequences. This would lead to many problems—as a simple example, imagine each driver's behaviors having to be shaped strictly by direct, actual consequences. Among rule-governed behaviors, Skinner includes the effects of commands, advice, warnings, directions, instructions, folklore, proverbs, governmental and religious laws, and the laws of science. Our behaviors come under the influence of rules because of reinforcement for following them. In other words, just as we "learn" other behaviors, we also learn to follow rules.)

Lastly, it's interesting to consider the following questions: "Even if Skinner's approach were judged to be simple, (which seems unjustified on the basis of what has been said above) is that necessarily bad? Is a complex approach inherently better than a simple one? Isn't it important to ask which approach is more useful and which one works better?" Skinnerian psychology has not yet proved itself to the point where all other approaches must immediately take a back seat, and it may indeed prove to be too simple to be *the* explanation for *all* of human behavior. On the other hand, its successful applications in a number of complex situations indicate increasing possibilities.

So far we have discussed common misunderstandings related to the four major sources of controversy covered in chapter 4. It is important to point out several additional ways in which Skinnerian psychology is sometimes misinterpreted. Specifically, we will consider the confusion of Skinner's approach with other approaches, and will touch on what Skinner has to say about some issues that many times are mistakenly thought to be ignored by him: feelings, thoughts, self-knowledge, self-control, and creativity.

SKINNER'S APPROACH
VERSUS OTHER METHODS
OF BEHAVIOR CONTROL

Skinner's emphasis when advocating behavior control is on the use of positive reinforcement. He suggests setting up environments in which persons behave in individually and socially beneficial ways because those behaviors are positively reinforced. Further, he recommends that we do this in a planned, systematic way, and not leave "good" behavior to chance. (It isn't that we completely ignore the use of positive reinforcement now, but rather that we often use it in a haphazard way.) In looking at what is going on presently in our society, Skinner sees that behavior often is controlled through aversive techniques and punishment. Instead of consistently and effectively using positive reinforcement to promote desirable and appropriate behaviors, those in positions of authority (teachers, parents, supervisors, employers, etc.) often resort to threats, reprimands, penalties, and so forth, in order to control the behavior of those under them. Of course, you don't necessarily have to be in a position of authority to use aversive and punishing techniques; these techniques sometimes are used in return against authority figures and also in relationships among peers. Skinner clearly is against using such techniques of behavior control and advises that we try to maximize the use of positive reinforcement rather than using it in a now-and-then, hit-or-miss fashion.

The significant point here is that Skinner's program for controlling behavior rests on the use of positive reinforcement. This is not always clearly understood. People sometimes confuse Skinner's approach with other, unrelated approaches. Numerous magazine and newspaper articles have made this error. For example, a recent article in a very popular news magazine equated Skinner's methods with those of putting prisoners in solitary confinement, giving child molesters severe electric shocks in the groin while showing them pictures of naked children, and giving a drug that causes severe vomiting to mentally disturbed inmates who were caught lying or swearing. It even went on to include brain surgery for the criminally insane as a technique of behavior modification. The article drew a direct connection between these methods and the suggestions of Skinner. Nothing could be further from the truth. He has specifically and plainly disavowed any association with such techniques. Despite this, erroneous conclusions continue to be drawn about what Skinner has suggested, and often there is no acknowledgment that his proposals for behavior control focus on positive reinforcement.

FEELINGS AND THOUGHTS

Another frequent misinterpretation of Skinnerian psychology is that it ignores feelings and thoughts. "All that Skinner talks about is behavior and the environment. He doesn't seem to believe that we have emotions or that we can think!" These types of comments are common. It's very true that he is a behaviorist, and a radical one at that. However, it isn't true that he denies the reality of feelings and thought processes. How could he? He himself has emotions and thoughts (despite what his more hostile critics have suggested). It would be rather absurd if he were to say that these inner states didn't exist. Though he acknowledges that we feel and think, Skinner does have a rather unique way of looking at these internal experiences. They have *no causal status* in his system of psychology.

Most of us believe that much of our behavior is determined by our feelings and thoughts. For example, someone might say, "I worked hard today because I was in a good mood" or "I stayed home yesterday because I was depressed." Skinner would not accept these explanations of behavior. He would accept the fact that this person felt "good" today and "depressed" yesterday, but he would not go along with the notion that these feelings *caused* the person to either work hard or stay home. To Skinner, feelings do not cause behavior. Rather, the specifics of both feelings and behavior are determined by environmental factors. Both "feeling good" and "working hard" can be controlled by positive reinforcers, such as adequate pay, praise from supervisors, regular promotions, good relationships with co-workers, and being able to do one's job effectively. Both "feeling depressed" and "staying home from work" can be controlled by aversive conditions, such as inadequate pay, criticism from supervisors, lack of recognition for good performance, poor relationships with co-workers, and inability to do one's job effectively. Skinner advises that these types of environmental factors provide the key to explaining both our feelings and our behaviors.

Thinking is also controlled by the environment. For example, a person growing up in a wealthy family in New York City will have quite different thoughts from those of someone growing up in a very isolated area with parents who are barely scratching out a living. Although a very obvious example, it makes the point that particular thoughts are shaped by the social and physical environments to which the individual is exposed.

Humans, because of the genetic characteristics of the species, are capable of feeling and thinking. These capabilities are givens; they exist because of their survival value during our evolutionary history. Just as we have the capabilities for speaking, reading, picking up objects with our fingers, walking upright, and so on, we also are capable of feeling and thinking. However, according to Skinner, the *extent* to which we feel and think, and *what* we feel and think about, are determined by environmental factors, especially the influence of other persons. They question us about our feelings and thoughts ("How do you feel today?" or "What are you thinking?") and reinforce our responses with their attention and comments. Thereby, the activities of feeling and thinking become important to us. Some persons may become more "sensitive" or "introspective" than others because engaging in these activities has been more strongly reinforced.

As mentioned, *what* we feel and think is also influenced by the significant persons in our lives. To give a very simple example, the victory of a Democratic presidential candidate is likely to cause feelings of happiness and thoughts of prosperity among the members of a politically involved family who happen to be Democrats; they encourage and reinforce each other's political feelings and beliefs. On the other hand, the members of a staunch Republican family would be likely to experience despair and thoughts of economic deprivation after the Democratic victory, because of their mutual encouragement and reinforcement of an alternative set of feelings and beliefs. Different environments result in differences in what is felt and thought.

The idea that feelings and thoughts control behavior is generally accepted in our society but is not accepted by Skinner. We easily accept explanations based on emotional and mental states: "She quit smoking because she wanted to"; "He's not going to the party because he feels sad"; "She finally decided to buy a car." These types of statements suggest that the reasons for behavior reside within the person. But we are left with having to explain why the first person "wants," why the second person is "sad," and why the third person "decided." Skinner would advise looking for the environmental conditions that are related to certain feelings or thoughts, as well as overt behaviors. A satisfactory explanation consists of finding the environmental events that control the ways we feel, think, *and* behave. (Actually, in Skinner's approach, feeling and thinking also can be considered behaviors. Though they occur "within the skin" and are not directly observable, they obey the same basic rules as our overt, public, observable behaviors; that is, they too are subject to environmental control.)

SELF-KNOWLEDGE

In contemporary society, we put a lot of emphasis on "knowing ourselves." It is commonly thought that to be able to understand our inner states is a strong virtue. Skinner suggests that there is a special problem in gaining this type of knowledge: Those around us can't directly observe our internal conditions and therefore can't help us to label them consistently. For example, it's quite a different matter to teach children to differentiate among colors, shapes, symbols, and so on, than it is to teach them to differentiate among the stimuli that arise within their bodies. In the latter case the stimuli are private, in the sense that others do not have direct access to them. These stimuli can only be inferred from what the individual says or does.

It is important to realize that Skinner does address the issue of self-knowledge, although he discusses it in materialistic, rather than spiritual, terms. For him, the problem of "knowing ourselves" has to do with stimuli, responses, and reinforcement. It is not a matter of getting in touch with some deep inner self or special internal quality.

Skinner approaches the topic of self-knowledge by identifying the three nervous systems by which we respond to our bodies: (1) the *interoceptive system* carries stimuli from our digestive, respiratory, and circulatory systems; (2) the *proprioceptive system* carries stimuli from muscles, joints, tendons, and other organs involved in body postures and movements; and (3) the *exteroceptive system* carries the stimuli received from our bodies and our surroundings that are involved in seeing, hearing, tasting, touching, and smelling. These three systems are assumed to have developed during our evolutionary history because of their biological significance, but with the development of verbal communication they came to serve a new function: to answer questions about ourselves.

When we are asked by others about our feelings, sensations, perceptions, thoughts, and so on, we learn to observe our bodily states in response to these questions. Therefore, what often is referred to as "self-knowledge" is essentially the result of observations that we make of interoceptive and proprioceptive stimuli arising from within our bodies. These self-observations are brought about initially by persons who inquire about our inner states and reinforce certain of our responses with attention and approval. (Skinner refers to these persons as the "verbal community"). If it weren't for these persons, there would be no self-knowledge. In short, Skinner suggests that observing and reporting on our inner states (more specifically, the stimuli that arise from our viscera, muscles, etc.) are *behaviors* that are shaped and maintained by the verbal community, and without this environmental influence there would be little reason to observe and report these internal events Of course, once self-observations have been reinforced we then often make them on our own, even in the absence of immediate influences from other persons.

To return to an earlier point, Skinner believes that accurate self-knowledge is difficult to acquire. Since the verbal community doesn't have direct access to the relevant stimuli, it can't consistently provide reinforcement for making distinctions among the various ways we "feel." If a teacher (a member of the verbal community) wants a child to differentiate between capital and lowercase letters, they both can look directly at the stimuli involved and the teacher can consistently reinforce the correct responses. However, if the teacher wants the child to differentiate between "sadness" and "loneliness," the situation is more complicated. Only the child has access to the internal stimuli that can be labeled either as "feeling sad" or "feeling lonely." The teacher has to guess what the child is experiencing, and therefore cannot consistently reinforce the child's distinctions. (Of course, if the external events that are affecting the child are known, the teacher can be more consistent.)

Because of this type of difficulty, Skinner suggests that we can't know what is going on inside of us as well as we can know external, objective events in the surrounding environment. Importantly, however, he believes that internal events "within the skin" and external events occurring in the world at large have a similar physical status. The former are simply "out of reach" for the verbal community, while they are immediate and intimate for the individual. Their immediacy and intimacy often result in the assignment of special qualities to inner stimuli, as though they define the "essence" or the "real personality" of the individual. Skinner obviously does not agree with such views of inner states.

For him, they are to be explained in the same way as overt events are explained: by referring to *stimuli*, *responses*, and the *consequences* that follow responses.

SELF-CONTROL

Skinner doesn't approach *self-control* in the traditional fashion. To Skinner, it isn't the exercise of "will power" nor does it involve "thinking through" a problem to come to a "rational decision" about the prudent course of action. Rather, it refers to behaviors that successfully change the probability of making some response. For example, some "self-controlling" behaviors reduce the chances of making a response that will be punished, and are reinforced by the fact that they *do* reduce punishable responses.

In self-control, one response (the *controlling* response) alters the factors that control another response (the *controlled* response). The controlled response may be one that has conflicting consequences. In other words, it is capable of producing both positive and negative outcomes. For example, drinking alcoholic beverages, smoking cigarettes, and overeating are responses that can have both reinforcing consequences (such as physical pleasure and escape from boring circumstances) and punishing consequences (such as physical disorders and social censure). We often vacillate between doing these things and not doing them. If the consequences of doing them became sufficiently aversive, we are apt to "control ourselves." A typical observer might explain our controlling behavior by referring to our "decision" to finally exert some "will power," but to Skinner the important determinant would be the aversive consequences that we escape or avoid.

Consider an example of a heavy smoker. He enjoys smoking, saying that it relaxes him, gives him a break from the routine at work, and in social situations gives him "something to do with his hands" (in other words, smoking has certain reinforcing outcomes for this person). On the other hand, he reads that smoking can cause heart and lung diseases, his doctor warns him about its ill effects and suggests that he stop, his wife tells him that she worries about his health and also dislikes the smell of stale cigarette butts, and he begins to have coughing spells and finds that he gets out of breath easily. What will he do? Skinner's reasoning suggests that his actions will be determined by these various influences, and that the idea of his "making a decision" to smoke or not smoke is illusory. If he quits and remains a nonsmoker it is because of the reduction of punishing, aversive outcomes; refraining from smoking may be additionally reinforced by praise from his doctor, wife, and friends, by renewed physical abilities, and in other ways.

Skinner suggests that it is of little use to urge people to use "will power" or to "take personal responsibility" for their behavior. He believes that these methods of encouraging self-control are not likely to have strong effects (though they may provide more aversive stimulation that the person can reduce through controlling behaviors, and in that way can sometimes contribute to self-control). According to Skinner, it is more effective to teach techniques for controlling undesirable behaviors. These techniques can be taught in the same way as any other skill, that is, by reinforcing appropriate responses. Individuals can learn to avoid tempting situations, to "do something else" that is incompatible with undesirable behavior (for example, an overweight person might exercise instead of eating), to use physical restraint (for example, a nail-biter might keep his hands in his pockets), and so on. Appropriate techniques of self-control need to be taught to each individual for his or her own particular problems.[2]

---

[2] There are a number of books that give details on how to use behavior modification techniques on oneself. Two of the better ones are: David L. Watson and Roland G. Tharp, *Self-Directed Behavior: Self-Modification for Personal Adjustment*, 2nd ed. (Monterey, Ca.: Brooks/Cole Publishing Company, 1977); and Robert L. Williams and James D. Long, *Toward a Self-Managed Life Style*, 2nd ed. (Boston: Houghton Mifflin Company, 1979).

Despite the common belief that Skinner has nothing to say about *creativity*, he does discuss it. Again, however, his reasoning isn't traditional. He doesn't account for creativity by referring to "creative impulses" or "ingenious uses of inner resources." As with other behaviors, Skinner suggests that creativity is the result of a person's genetic endowment and environmental experiences.

When someone does something "creative" (for example, invents a new tool, discovers a new solution for an old problem, paints a beautiful picture, or writes an inspiring poem) we often think that he or she has some special inner quality. Skinner's analysis points instead toward special experiences that have interacted with the person's genetic endowment to produce unique behaviors. Therefore, instead of giving the person credit, his or her environment deserves credit.

Though creative acts sometimes seem somewhat mysterious, as though they occur spontaneously and almost impulsively, it must be remembered that the persons involved generally have complex histories of reinforcement for a wide variety of behaviors. Many situations in which creativity takes place are not totally new or unfamiliar. Even in situations where there seems to be little similarity with the person's previous experiences, there may be subtle common elements to which the person responds. If the individual has a large behavioral repertoire relevant to the project at hand, he or she will "try out" various behaviors until a "creative act" finally emerges.

An observer might notice only the final behavioral product and admire the sudden act of creativity. This is understandable, because the process leading to it sometimes occurs very quickly. Much of the process may occur covertly, since on the basis of previous experiences the creative person can think about various possible behaviors and their outcomes. "Thinking" in this sense is simply behaving, but at a level at which it can't be observed by others. (Remember, Skinner doesn't deny thought processes; he believes, however, that the specifics of what we think about are determined by our experiences, that our thoughts are not "free," and that thinking is not a cause of behavior. Thinking may serve as a substitute for carrying out behaviors at the overt level; it is essentially similar, but occurs "inside the skin.")

Some creative behaviors do occur quite spontaneously and don't necessarily follow the process just mentioned. To explain these behaviors, Skinner refers to "mutations" and selection. He likens his ideas to those of Darwin's theory of evolution. During the evolutionary process, certain genetic mutations are selected because of their survival value. In a similar sense, certain behavioral mutations occur and are selected because they are successful (reinforcing). For example, an artist who uses a different brush stroke or an inventor who changes the design of a machine are producing mutations that may survive (be selected) if they are "pleasing" or "useful" (that is, if they are reinforcing).

Mutations can result from "accidents" (such as when an artist picks up the wrong brush and begins using it or when an inventor makes a beneficial mistake in design) or they can be variations due to the reinforcement involved in "doing things differently." In the latter case, there are artists, inventors, musicians, writers, and other creative individuals who have received attention and praise for varying their approaches, and therefore they continue to be "creative" by exploring new ground. Also, they may be reinforced simply by the new effects that their creative behaviors produce (that is, the reinforcements are not necessarily social ones).

Skinner suggests that creative persons have been exposed to environmental circumstances that have molded their creativity. According to him, we do what we do, creative or not, because of the consequences of our behaviors or because of consequences that have been described to us. Creative behaviors are impressive because of their novelty and often they make the average person feel that "I never could have done that because I'm just not that original or unique." What may be missing for the average person, however, is not some special inner quality, but rather some "original" or "unique" past and present environmental circumstances. If the creative person's experiences could be duplicated exactly, in all their subtle as well as obvious details, it is likely that creativity would also be duplicated (assuming that genetic endowments didn't differ significantly). But would it then still be "creativity?"

This chapter has been concerned with misunderstandings about Skinnerian psychology. To summarize some of the major points: (1) Skinner opposes the traditional concept of self-determination, but he supports the ideals of individual achievement and satisfaction within a strong society; (2) he is a determinist, but acknowledges the possibilities of unpredictability and the meaningfulness of individual actions; (3) he strongly advocates the systematic control of behavior through control of environmental factors, but also emphasizes the need for countercontrol; (4) he initially developed his concepts of behavior from rat and pigeon studies, but many applications at the human level have been successful; (5) his concept of positive reinforcement may appear simplistic, but its applications are broad and often lead to the learning of complex behaviors; (6) his approach to behavior control emphasizes the use of positive reinforcement, and does *not* advocate aversive control, punishment, or brain surgery as means of controlling behaviors; (7) he suggests that particular feelings and thoughts are *not* causes of behavior, but rather are themselves determined (in a manner similar to overt behaviors) by environmental conditions; (8) he explains self-knowledge, self-control, and creativity in behavioral terms, emphasizing that these activities are controlled by environmental conditions (mainly by behavioral *consequences*), rather than resulting from personal inner qualities or states of mind.

SIX

WHAT DOES SKINNER SAY ABOUT SIGMUND FREUD?

B. F. Skinner was born in 1904, grew up in the small American town of Susquehanna, Pennsylvania, graduated from Harvard University's doctoral program in psychology, devoted much of his life to laboratory research, and is an advocate of radical behaviorism. Sigmund Freud was born in 1856, grew up in the European city of Vienna, graduated from the University of Vienna's medical school, spent much of his life analyzing mental disorders, and was the founder of psychoanalysis. What do these two men of such different backgrounds have in common?

Both have had tremendous impacts on the field of psychology, have gained widespread public attention, and have stirred up a large amount of controversy by challenging the traditional views of their times. In addition, they share these characteristics: (1) *intense interest in understanding behavior;* whether it be Skinner's rats pressing levers or Freud's patients telling their dreams, attention is devoted to the causes of behavior; (2) *emphasis on the study of individual organisms, rather than groups;* though both have written about group behavior, Skinner's laboratory research focused on the behaviors of individual rats or pigeons isolated in Skinner boxes, while Freud concentrated on individual patients undergoing analysis in the privacy of his office; (3) *concern with the extension of their findings to social problems;* despite the fact that the research of both focused on individual organisms, their writings reflect great interest in applying their findings to the larger levels of society, in fact, to society as a whole; (4) *belief that humans essentially are not rational decision-makers;* Skinner believes that it is our genes and the environment, rather than rational decisions, that cause us to behave as we do, and Freud believed that we are strongly influenced by unconscious, irrational motives; (5) *belief that behavior is determined in a lawful way by natural causes;* rather than believing that behaviors occur haphazardly or mysteriously, they both stress that there is an underlying orderliness determined by the nature of humans and the world in which we live.

Though Skinner and Freud share some common characteristics, there also are some striking differences. These differences will become clear in the following sections, as we take a look at what Skinner has said about Freud. He has set himself apart from Freud in a number of important ways. Here and there, I have used examples that I believe accurately represent Skinner's meanings.

THE "MENTAL APPARATUS"

Skinner has written that an important contribution of Freud was to reduce "the sphere of accident and caprice in our considerations of human conduct."[1] In other words, he was a determinist, and Skinner agrees with the value of this approach. Freud analyzed many behaviors that previously were thought either too insignificant to consider or too complex to explain. He found reasons for minor behaviors such as slips of the tongue, errors in writing, and the forgetting of names or appointments, as well as more dramatic behaviors such as fainting, nightmares, losing the use of a limb despite the absence of a physical problem, and uncontrollable fears of harmless animals or objects. He took the approach that naturalistic explanations are possible. He didn't give up easily and simply say something like: "Well, I guess there's no way of explaining that; it's just something mysterious that happens."

[1] B. F. Skinner, "A Critique of Psychoanalytic Concepts and Theories," in *Cumulative Record: A Selection of Papers*, 3rd ed. (New York: Appleton-Century-Crofts, 1972), p. 239.

While praising Freud's determination to find the causes of various behaviors, Skinner suggests that he spent too much time looking in the wrong place. Freud's wasted efforts, in Skinner's view, were due to his construction of a "mental apparatus" to account for behavior. This apparatus consists primarily of the well-known triad—id, ego, and superego. The *id* refers to primitive human nature: the basic instincts and repressed, irrational wishes and impulses, all of which are unconscious. The *ego* is the realistic aspect of the personality. It attempts to satisfy the id's demands while also meeting the requirements of reality and the moral prescriptions of the *superego*, which includes the conscience. Freud often referred to these internal systems when explaining behavior. The id's instincts could result in impulsive behavior, the ego's realistic processes could result in rational behavior, and the superego could cause moralistic behavior.

It isn't completely clear how Freud meant these internal personality mechanisms to be used. He varied his own usage of them. In some of his writings, it seems that the id is meant to stand for human genetic inheritance, while the ego and superego refer to what persons learn as they are socialized. In other writings, Freud slips away from this usage, and the id, ego, and superego assume a reality of their own, as though they actually exist within the person and determine behavior.

According to Skinner, there is an inherent danger in using mentalistic concepts for explaining behavior. They tend to become *the* explanations, in and of themselves. In actuality, they can never be real explanations, because they themselves have to be explained. (Skinner calls such concepts "explanatory fictions"— they seem to explain behavior, but in fact explain nothing). If persons are said to do things because of irrational wishes of the id, rational ideas of the ego, or moralistic values of the superego, the question remains as to how the wishes, ideas, and values originated. That question carries the explanation back to environmental influences (some experience or set of experiences that the person has had) or to some genetic factor. To Skinner, one's environmental experiences and genetic endowment are the determinants that have to be taken into account, and mentalistic concepts get in the way of the pursuit of these critical factors. (Though including genetic factors as behavioral determinants, Skinner himself has concentrated on the study of environmental factors, because they are more directly observable, are more easily altered, and have the strongest effects on the specifics of behavior.)

Skinner suggests that Freud's failure to stick with environmental determinism, and his commitment to a determinism that mixes mentalistic concepts with environmental factors, has resulted in considerable damage. Though Freud seemed at times to recognize the dangers of using concepts such as id, ego, and superego, he chose to use them anyway. As a result his and his followers' pursuit of environmental determinants of behavior has been seriously hindered. Skinner explains this by noting that the Freudian explanatory system involves three steps: (1) an *external environmental event* (some experience) produces (2) an *internal mental state* (such as an emotion, idea, or conflict) that results in (3) some *observable behavior.* For example, certain traumatic environmental events of early childhood can produce long-lasting inner conflicts that can cause adult neurotic behaviors.

What's wrong with this three-link causal chain? Skinner illustrates the problem with an example of *punishment* for childhood sexual behavior, which produces *anxiety or guilt*, that then supposedly causes *unusual adult sexual behaviors.* He believes that the middle link isn't needed and, furthermore, it confuses matters. For him, the actual explanation for the adult's unusual sexual behaviors is the punishment incident, not the anxiety or guilt (they too would be caused by the punishment—they are not causes themselves, but effects). By introducing the middle link of anxiety or guilt, attention tends to get drawn away from the antecedent environmental event (punishment).

Also, Skinner points out that inner states such as anxiety or guilt have a tendency to steal the *whole* show. Not only do they detract from the investigation of environmental events, but they cloud the detailed study of the behavioral outcomes of these

events. In other words, anxiety or guilt becomes so central that
the important question of exactly what the person is *doing* (or not
doing) gets slighted. Specifically, in our example, it is important
to know precisely what the unusual sexual behaviors are, how
often they occur, and under what circumstances they occur. This
type of information clarifies the problem. If anxiety, guilt, or
some other inner state becomes the center of attention, it is easy
to forget to observe the details of the problem behavior.

Skinner is disturbed by what he feels is a general tendency
for us to look *within* for answers to our behavioral problems and
he feels that Freud contributed greatly to this tendency. How
many times have you heard someone discuss anxieties, fears,
inner conflicts, and so on? We frequently use these kinds of concepts to explain our own behaviors as well as those of other persons. But are we really explaining anything, or are we using "explanatory fictions?" Wouldn't it clarify things and be more helpful
to focus on the specific observable behaviors that indicate what
we call anxiety, fear, or conflict, rather than referring to some
vague, unobservable inner state? Second, wouldn't it be beneficial
to consider how the environment can be changed to bring about
more desirable behaviors? Skinner advocates this two-step process, rather than the three-step process of Freud. For Skinner, it is
essential to identify the relationships between environmental
factors and behaviors. He sees Freud as having confused things by
insisting on an intermediate mental apparatus.

Does this mean that Skinner ignores our mental states and
denies that we feel, think, have doubts, suffer from anxieties and
guilt, and so on? The answer, as has been made clear in other
sections of this book, is "No." He acknowledges that we experience these states, but he doesn't see them as being in the causal
chain. *They are effects, not causes.* The specifics of what we feel
and think are controlled by environmental conditions, just as
overt observable behaviors are.

Skinner has pointed out two major problems that arise if
mentalistic concepts are considered as explanations of behavior.
First, *how can mental states be observed?* They cannot be studied

objectively. This is a serious issue in developing a science of behavior. Of course, mental states can be inferred from what people
say they are thinking or feeling, but such statements often are
inconsistent and have doubtful accuracy. Skinner suggests that
behavioral scientists should look directly for the environmental
conditions that affect behavior, rather than looking for causes in
the inner experiencing of those conditions. According to his view,
persons react to the environment, not to their inner states. These
inner states exist, but they too are environmentally influenced.

Second, *how can mental states by altered directly?* This is an
important question for psychoanalysts and other therapists, since
they often focus on changing their patients' feelings, thoughts,
expectations, and other inner states. (For example, Freud emphasized the necessity of developing the inner quality of "a strong
ego.") In Skinner's view, there is no such thing as *directly*
changing an inner state. If patients develop better feelings and
clearer thoughts it is because their environmental conditions and
behaviors have changed, regardless of what the therapist or patient believes is the cause of the improvement. Therapy sessions
themselves may provide a changed environment, and therapists
additionally may suggest things that patients can do in their
everyday lives to alter their situations. Skinner's reasoning suggests that these changes actually are the factors that bring therapeutic results, even though they may seem incidental or secondary
in importance to the therapist's goal of working on the patient's
feelings or thinking processes.

Following Skinner's advice, it would be most efficient to go
directly to environmental factors and behaviors, instead of complicating the therapeutic process by attempting to deal with the
patient's inner states. "Take care of the person's environment and
behavior and his (her) inner condition will take care of itself" is
one way of putting Skinner's theme. When using techniques based
on Skinner's ideas, behavior therapists help their clients improve
their circumstances, behaviors, and behavioral consequences
(that is, they try to change the "contingencies of reinforcement").
When these factors improve, better feelings and thoughts also are

likely to occur. As a simple example, receiving positive reinforcement (such as approval from the therapist or others) not only can shape and strengthen improved behaviors but can produce "good feelings." As the client progresses, more and more effective behaviors develop; these behaviors, and the consequences they produce, help to sustain the client's "healthy mental and emotional state."

Skinner's criticisms of Freud's use of mentalistic concepts are not meant to completely negate Freud's accomplishments. Freud made many interesting observations that connected childhood experiences to adult behaviors and Skinner appreciates the importance of these observations. Also, he acknowledges that patients sometimes improve during psychoanalysis or related therapies. However, he suggests that rather than being explained by psychoanalytic notions, these successes are related to the altering of the patient's environment and behavior. For example, for the first time the patient may be in a situation in which he can say anything he wants without being criticized or judged. The fact that the analyst provides a "nonpunishing audience" may be a critical environmental factor that determines the patient's "cure."

Skinner's main point is that Freud would have been *more* effective in both theorizing and doing therapy, and his ideas would have led to *less* confusion and wasted effort, if he had never used mentalistic concepts. In Skinner's opinion, Freud should have stuck to the study of the details of behavior (how, when, and where does it occur) and to the consequences of those behaviors. (In essence, Skinner is saying that Freud should have been a behaviorist.)

THE UNCONSCIOUS

Another aspect of Freudian psychology that Skinner has criticized is the concept of the *unconscious mind*. Freud divided the mind into three levels of consciousness: (1) the *conscious*, which includes all that we are aware of at a particular time, (2) the *preconscious*, which consists of material that can be brought to the conscious level relatively easily if we concentrate on it, and (3) the *unconscious*, which contains material of which we are unaware but that nevertheless affects our behavior. It is the unconscious, according to Freud, that primarily dominates our personalities. It contains instinctive sexual and aggressive impulses, forbidden wishes and desires, unpleasant memories, and other elements that churn away below the surface and push us in various directions. (There is overlap between the concepts of the unconscious and the id. The id is considered to be totally unconscious and therefore the reservoir of much of the material at that level.) Freud's psychoanalytic techniques are designed to tap the unconscious, so that disturbing material can be revealed and "worked through" (which involves coming to terms with long-hidden impulses, wishes, conflicts, etc.). The two main techniques that Freud used to accomplish this were *dream interpretation* (psychoanalysts consider dreams to be indicators of unconscious wishes) and *free association* (the patient is told to relax and to say whatever comes to mind—this is intended to allow unconscious material to surface gradually).

Skinner considers the unconscious to be a misleading concept. He objects primarily to Freud's idea that the unconscious has a *causal* role in determining behavior, a central theme in Freud's theory of human behavior and his psychoanalytic therapy. Skinner maintains that behavior is determined by genetic and environmental factors, and that there is no reason to assign special importance to the person's state of awareness regarding these factors. We are aware (conscious) of some of these factors and unaware (unconscious) of others, but the implication of Skinner's line of reasoning is "So what?" To him, our awareness or lack of awareness of the genetic and environmental factors that influence us is incidental, *having no causal significance.*

Simply stated, Skinner suggests that it doesn't matter whether or not we are aware of the factors that act on us; they still exist and have an effect. Therefore, Freud's elevation of the unconscious to a position of unique significance is unwarranted. It causes misplaced efforts to "analyze" the unconscious, when what really needs "analyzing" are the genetic and (especially) the environmental factors that cause individuals to behave as they do. The degree of awareness that people have about these factors is not what causes their behaviors. In fact, according to Skinner, awareness itself is a type of behavior; thus, it is an effect rather than a cause.

To give an example, among some people there is great emphasis on "knowing yourself." Questions such as "How do you feel about that?" or "What are you thinking?" are asked often, and certain responses are reinforced with attention and approval. Similarly, from a Skinnerian perspective, a psychoanalyst attempts to get patients to become more aware of their experiencing of past and present environmental conditions, and reinforces them with attention and approval (perhaps by mentioning that progress is being made) when they make appropriate descriptive statements about this experiencing. In this way, what was previously "unconscious" becomes "conscious." Skinner acknowledges that people are capable of some degree of self-awareness (self-observation) because of human genetic inheritance, but he believes that this type of behavior actually occurs only when it is encouraged and reinforced by our fellow human beings (the "verbal community"). Some persons become more "aware" than others because they have more experiences in which awareness is reinforced.

It's interesting to consider that both Skinner and Freud would agree that we don't have to be aware of our behavior or its determinants in order to carry out actions. All of us do certain things without consciously knowing why we do them, sometimes without even realizing what we are doing. When our attention is called to such actions, we might say that we do them "automatically," "without thinking," "impulsively," or we might even deny that we do them at all. Though both Skinner and Freud agree that such behaviors exist, they disagree about their importance.

To review and summarize Skinner's position, he suggests

simply that sometimes we are aware of our behavior and its causes, and sometimes we are not, depending on what our experiences have been. Some persons are encouraged frequently by others (such as parents, peers, or psychoanalysts) to observe their own behaviors and doing so is often reinforced. Therefore, the behaviors of being aware of what they are doing and why they are doing it become conditioned, and they make more self-observations than those who have had fewer such experiences. In either case, Skinner would argue that awareness is not a determinant of behavior. It is itself a behavior and is subject to the same rules as other behaviors: if making self-observations (being aware) is reinforced, it will continue to occur.

Freud, on the other hand, chose to place the unconscious at the center of both his theorizing and his analytic procedures with patients. In his view, unconscious factors affect the behaviors of both normal and neurotic individuals to varying extents, though his main focus was on neurotic behaviors. He believed that to overcome negative unconscious influences, we must develop an awareness of these disturbing elements, and this could occur adequately only through the process of psychoanalysis. By bringing disturbing *unconscious* material to the *conscious* level, and then "working it through" to remove its irrational, emotional grip on us, we can change our neurotic behaviors. It's clear that Freud felt that it can make a difference in our behavior if we become aware of previously unconscious factors, and this is a point on which he and Skinner disagree. Skinner has suggested that such awareness is not critical, and that our behaviors are affected by environmental and genetic factors, whether or not awareness of these factors exists. (Currently, this is a controversial issue, even among behaviorists. There is evidence indicating that certain self-monitoring or self-observation procedures can influence behavior. For example, sometimes simply counting and keeping a record of the frequency of a certain behavior—smoking, eating, swearing, etc.—can affect its frequency. These procedures often are taught by behavior therapists and behavior modifiers. However, they are considered as useful behaviors that clients are capable of learning, and not as methods for "probing the unconscious" or "discovering underlying conflicts.")

Related to this issue, Skinner suggests that Freud's own observation that we can be affected by unconscious factors (such as forgotten traumatic childhood incidents and biological events within our bodies) could have lead Freud to the more general conclusion that degree of awareness is *not* a causal factor in determining behavior. In other words, if we can be influenced by factors of which we are unaware, then awareness itself should not be a critical factor. However, that is not what Freud concluded and it is not what guided his efforts. He made strong distinctions between conscious and unconscious processes, and indicated that significant behavioral outcomes were related to these different states. But this opened up another question: By what specific mechanism do states of awareness affect behavior? In Skinner's opinion, Freud did not supply an adequate answer.

Skinner's advice is to look for environmental determinants of our behaviors, but such determinants are less exciting and dramatic than are Freud's. Our cultural experiences have made guilt, anxiety, uncontrollable impulses, hidden desires, forbidden wishes, and other presumably unconscious motives for behavior much more stimulating to consider and discuss. The greatest disadvantage of our interest in these types of explanations, in Skinner's opinion, is that they are "explanatory fictions"—we explain nothing by referring to these inner states. However fascinating they may be, they too have to be explained, and that requires the hard work of considering how our genes and experiences have brought these states into being.

DEFENSE MECHANISMS

In Freudian psychology, defense mechanisms are devices that are used unconsciously by the ego to cope with anxiety. Essentially, their use (especially if they are used extensively for a prolonged period) indicates a weak ego that is incapable of dealing realistically with the impulses and wishes of the id, the moralistic demands of the superego, and the external pressures from the environment. These forces can generate increasing amounts of anxiety if they aren't handled in some rational way. The inadequate ego therefore has to resort to the use of unrealistic, irrational defenses to try to deal with this anxiety. Defense mechanisms involve distortions or denials of the actual internal or external conditions that exist for the person. Skinner believes that the behaviors that Freud would have called "defensive" can be explained without referring to some action of an inner ego. Once again, Skinner relies on external environmental conditions to explain behavior, whereas Freud referred to inner processes. Let's consider briefly three of the Freudian defense mechanisms and the explanation that Skinner gives of each.

Repression was said by Freud to be the "cornerstone" or "foundation stone" of psychoanalysis. As a defense mechanism, it refers to the exclusion of unpleasant thoughts, experiences, impulses, and other material from consciousness, and explains why persons refrain from certain actions. For example, it might be said of someone that "He is repressing his desire to have an extramarital affair." Skinner suggests that the so-called effects of repression can be explained by referring to punishment. If persons have been punished or are under the threat of punishment for some behavior, they can avoid aversive consequences by not engaging in the forbidden behavior (such as an extramarital relationship) and by avoiding even the thought of it. For Skinner, it is unnecessary and misleading to use the concept of repression; external conditions (punishment or the threat of punishment) can explain why someone avoids doing or thinking about certain things.

Reaction formation is a defense mechanism that involves doing the opposite (often to an extreme) of what is unconsciously felt or thought. For example, unconscious resentment of a friend may be replaced with exaggerated displays of affection, or hidden sexual impulses may be covered up by extreme concern about morality. The ego supposedly attempts to protect against the anxiety that would result if the real feelings came to the surface. In Skinner's view, however, people respond to environmental circumstances, and it isn't necessary to bring in the concept of the ego using a "reaction formation." Basically, the individual will behave in ways that reduce the chances of being punished. If the threat of punishment is severe or persistent, action may be taken to "make certain" that the punishable behavior does not occur. In the first example above, dramatic displays of affection toward a friend make resentful behavior unlikely and punishing outcomes (loss of the friendship, bitter reprisals, etc.) are avoided. Also, it is likely that affectionate behaviors will be reinforced by the friend's positive reactions. In the second example, constant expressions of moral concern make sexual opportunities unlikely to be presented, and therefore a recurrence of punishment (that perhaps occurred during childhood) is avoided. Also, expressions of moral concern may be reinforced by attention and affirmation from others. In these explanations, individuals are seen as being controlled by environmental circumstances, primarily the consequences of particular behaviors, rather than being influenced by the inner workings of their egos.

Sublimation is a defense mechanism which, compared to repression, reaction formation, and others, has more positive benefits for the person and society. Freud suggested that the advance of culture is based on sublimation. The ego directs the energy of unconscious impulses into productive and creative activities. Basic sexual and aggressive drives are diverted into work and artistic pursuits, as well as other socially desirable behaviors. By accomplishing this, the ego reduces the buildup of tensions at the unconscious level and thereby lessens anxiety. Simply put, sublimation involves "draining off" unconscious energy by using it for constructive purposes.

Obviously, Skinner doesn't go along with this explanation based on inner, ego-directed processes. He suggests that being deprived of opportunities to emit reinforced behavior may strengthen similar behaviors. For example, if deprived of opportunities for sexual behavior, the person may paint pictures of the human body. Also, deprivation may strengthen the same behavior in similar stimulus situations, as when a childless couple treats a pet as if it were a child. In the presence of a stimulus (the pet) that bears certain similarities to a child (they both require care), the couple emits parental behavior. Where Freud was likely to see "sublimations of unconscious wishes," Skinner is likely to see conditions of deprivation and the generalization of responses (as in the case of painting pictures instead of engaging in sexual activities) or stimuli (as in the case when the stimulus "pet" has effects similar to the stimulus "child").

Skinner also has indicated that if two types of behavior (perhaps sexual activity and athletic performance) have been reinforced, and one of them is then punished, the other is more likely to occur. This is another possible explanation of some instances that Freud might have considered as sublimations of energy into alternative activities.

Persons who devote enormous amounts of time to their work might be considered as "sublimating" in Freud's terms, but they could also be viewed as individuals whose work behaviors are being positively reinforced by money, by the outcomes of their efforts (for example, writers who are reinforced by seeing the written pages in front of them), by the attention and approval of others, or by some other form of reinforcement. Skinner also offers another explanation: Many people work hard in order to escape negative consequences such as criticism or lack of money to buy essential goods. Again, we have the distinction between Freud's *inner* determinants and Skinner's *environmental* determinants.

PSYCHOTHERAPY

Skinner acknowledges Freud's strong impact on current therapeutic methods. As indicated earlier, he believes that therapists influenced by Freud typically represent a "nonpunishing audience." They avoid criticizing or judging their patients. As therapy progresses, patients behave more and more in ways that they have avoided previously. They may recall unpleasant memories, be critical of other persons (including the therapist), act in hostile or selfish ways, cry, have violent outbursts, and so on. If the therapist continues to be nonpunishing, feelings such as guilt, fear, and anxiety may gradually diminish and undesirable behaviors may decrease.

This behavioral explanation of the effectiveness of "traditional" psychotherapies (that is, Freudian and related therapies) is based on the following assumptions: Many persons who seek therapy have emotional and behavioral problems caused by the widespread use of punishment and aversive control in our society. Authority figures (such as parents, teachers, and employers), social institutions (such as religious organizations and government agencies), and one's associates as well, often rely on the use of punishment or threatened punishment to control behavior. Especially likely to produce problems for the individual are excessive or inconsistent uses of these controlling techniques. The traditional therapist provides a unique experience for such persons by being *consistently nonpunishing.* Troublesome emotions, and undesirable behaviors that the patient has used to escape and avoid aversive conditions, are thereby allowed to extinguish. To put it very simply, these undesirable emotional and behavioral responses subside when conditions make them unnecessary, and the nonpunishing therapist helps to establish those conditions.

Clearly, Skinner believes that the problems most patients bring to therapy result from the detrimental environmental conditions to which they have been exposed. What therapists need to do, in his view, is help construct new conditions for their patients that will bring about and maintain beneficial *behavioral* changes, which will have the accompanying effect of improving patients' emotional responses. He suggests that even though traditional therapies are sometimes helpful, they aren't based on this view of the therapist's task. According to Skinner: "The field of psychotherapy is rich in explanatory fictions."[2] Problem *behavior* is not examined as important subject matter in and of itself, but rather is thought of as an indication of some underlying disorder, often referred to as a "neurosis." Thus, the patient's neurosis (an explanatory fiction) is treated, rather than the patient's behavior.

Freud fostered the belief that unusual behavior is merely the symptom of an inner neurotic condition that must be removed if behavior is to be changed. This reasoning is similar to that of the physician who treats an infection in order to cure its symptoms, and often it is referred to as the "disease model" or the "medical model" of mental illness. Skinner says that "this doctrine has given psychotherapy an impossible assignment;"[3] the assumed "inner cause" can't be observed objectively and can't be altered directly. It is the so-called "symptoms" (the actual behaviors) that need to be worked on, not the internal states. By suggesting this, Skinner does not ignore the emotions of the person; by working on observable behaviors, the circumstances under which behaviors occur, and the consequences of behaviors, emotions will also be affected. In other words, environmental and behavioral changes are accompanied by emotional changes. This view differs from that of Freud, who saw emotions as *causes* of behavior. To Skinner, both overt behavior and inner emotional responses are products of environmental influences.

The therapeutic techniques advocated by Freud are aimed at rooting out the inner source of the patient's problems. Skinner points out the similarity between this and the notion that unusual behavior is due to "possession" by the Devil, and that the Devil must be exorcised from the body before the person can be cured. Instead of the Devil, there are "anxieties, conflicts, repressed wishes, and repressed memories" in Freudian psychology, and these must be discovered and resolved so that the patient's be-

---

[2] B. F. Skinner, *Science and Human Behavior* (New York: The Free Press, Collier-Macmillan Limited, 1953), pp. 372–373.

[3] Skinner, *Science and Human Behavior*, p. 373.

havioral symptoms will be relieved.[4] While doing this, the therapist also brings about changes in the patient's environment. Skinner believes that the patient is benefited by these *incidental* changes, rather than by the rooting out of inner problems.

Instead of relying on the effectiveness of incidental changes, Skinner suggests the systematic use of behavioral procedures to locate and change the environmental factors that are related to troublesome, maladaptive behaviors. To do this, therapists need to get away from the traditional idea of underlying neuroses and adopt the view that problem behaviors are strongly influenced by their consequences and accompanying environmental conditions. This view leads to the next step: helping persons change their circumstances, behaviors, and the reinforcing consequences of their behaviors (the interrelationships among these three factors are called "contingencies of reinforcement").

Behaviors that are maladaptive or troublesome may need to be *extinguished*. During therapy sessions or in the person's everyday life, situations can be set up so that these behaviors are no longer reinforced. At the same time, more desirable behaviors can be shaped through *positive reinforcement*. These goals often are accomplished by clients themselves, upon advice from a behavior therapist or behavior modifier. Here again, the concept of "rule-governed" behavior (discussed in chapter 5) is important: The client's behavior may be changed by the therapist's advice or suggestions. If these changes are reinforced, the progress of therapy will be facilitated. In common terms, the client will "trust" the therapist and continue to go along with his or her advice.

Looking briefly at a hypothetical case, suppose a person comes for therapy because he is having troubles with his wife, his job, and his social relationships. He complains a great deal and says that he feels very anxious at times, with depression and guilt at other times. A traditional therapist would be likely to focus a good deal of attention on the anxiety, depression, and guilt, believing these disturbed inner states to be, in strong measure, the

[4]Skinner, *Science and Human Behavior*, p. 374.

causes of the person's problem behaviors. *Behavior therapists* (many of whom have been influenced by Skinner's suggestions) commonly have a different perspective, viewing anxiety, depression, and guilt as the results of aversive environmental factors, rather than as causes of problems. These therapists tend to pinpoint specific behaviors that need to be changed and tend not to focus on inner states. In the case being discussed, a behavior therapist might gather details on the ways in which the man interacts with others, and then have him rehearse better ways of interacting, while *reinforcing* his progress with attention and approval. Meanwhile, the therapist might help to *extinguish* the man's unconstructive complaining by not encouraging it when it occurs and by changing to constructive discussions and the practicing of effective behavior. Additionally, the therapist would be likely to help him plan various changes in his everyday life, in order to bring about more constructive, adaptive behaviors and to ensure the reinforcement of such behaviors.

A question might be: "What happens to the anxiety, depression, and guilt?" Skinner's reasoning is that discomforting feelings will change when the person's circumstances, behaviors, and behavioral consequences change. Anxiety, depression, and guilt commonly result from an individual's history of poor behavioral consequences. For example, if someone has been unsuccessful in his or her interpersonal relationships, a number of punishing outcomes for behaviors have occurred, producing behavioral and emotional problems. When the person becomes more successful, that is, when behaviors are learned that bring positive reinforcement instead of punishment, better feelings will result.

Finally, does the therapeutic approach advocated by Skinner deal *only* with symptoms rather than basic, underlying causes? This is a question that has been raised by Freudian therapists who feel that behavior therapy is superficial. They believe that there is an internal cause for emotional and behavioral problems, and that this cause must be discovered and dealt with before the person can expect permanent relief. Though admitting that behavior therapists may temporarily improve their patients, they argue that "symptom substitution" is likely. That is, a problem behavior may be changed, but some other problem will emerge because the underlying conflict, repressed trauma, or other basic cause, has not been treated. (This argument is based on the "disease model," mentioned earlier). Skinner doesn't give any weight to this line of reasoning. He believes that, like it or not, a therapist always ends up dealing with basic *environmental factors* and *behavioral changes*, even when he or she thinks that "underlying problems" are being treated. (As a last note to this discussion of symptom substitution: Behavior therapists in recent years have conducted a number of studies to see whether new or different symptoms emerge when a problem behavior is removed or altered. The evidence indicates that symptom substitution, if it does occur, certainly is not obvious. In short, there is little if any research support for this notion.)

In summary, Skinner and Freud have some things in common. The writings of both indicate: (1) an intense interest in understanding behavior, (2) an emphasis on the study of individual organisms, (3) a concern with extending their findings to social problems, (4) a belief that humans are not essentially rational, and (5) a belief in lawful, naturalistic causes of behavior. There are several differences, however, that highlight the split between radical behaviorism and psychoanalysis. Skinner has been critical of Freud's (1) use of a "mental apparatus" to explain behavior, (2) distinction between conscious and unconscious states of awareness, (3) concept of defense mechanisms, and (4) assumptions regarding psychotherapy. These differences result mainly from Skinner's focus on external, observable environmental causes of behavior versus Freud's emphasis on the importance of inner emotional and mental states.

SEVEN

WHAT ARE THE DISAGREEMENTS BETWEEN SKINNER AND THE HUMANISTS?

THE HUMANISTIC REACTION

The humanistic movement in psychology grew by leaps and bounds during the 1960s, partially as a reaction against both psychoanalysis and behaviorism, and it is still influential. Abraham Maslow, one of its founders, called it the "third force" in psychology. "Humanism" or "humanistic psychology" is not easy to define precisely (distinctions could be made between these two terms, but for the purposes of this chapter they will be considered synonymous.) The many psychologists who group themselves under this heading hold a variety of viewpoints, though there are also certain commonalities among them. In contrast to Skinner's emphasis on the controlling influences of environmental factors, humanists insist that the most significant determinants of human behavior are certain inner qualities such as free will and subjective experiencing. While acknowledging that environmental factors affect us and that these factors can either enhance or inhibit our basic potentialities, humanists believe that at the core of humanness is a unique essence, a creative force, a will to grow and develop in fulfilling ways.

Though humanists are similar to Freudians in their belief that inner states are important determinants of human behavior (and can be criticized by Skinner for this in a way similar to his criticisms of Freud—see chapter 6), they are strikingly different in their emphasis on conscious and rational decision-making processes and in their optimistic view of basic human nature. They stress that people are essentially sociable, rational, and good, while Freudians tend to see strong elements of selfishness, irrationality, and destructive aggressiveness in human nature. (In the humanist sense, "rationality" typically refers to a reasonable or sensible approach to life situations, based on personal feelings and other inner experiencing, as well as considerations of the external environment. It does not refer to highly intellectualized thought processes.)

Humanists often react strongly to Skinner's ideas. They consider him to be the prime mover of a type of behaviorism that violates much of what they believe about human nature and the true meanings of human behavior. Skinner shows no respect for concepts such as free will, purposeful action, self-actualization, and inner meaning, which humanists feel are vital for understanding the essence of human existence and actions.

SKINNER AND CARL ROGERS: FRIENDLY FOES

The controversy between humanists and behaviorists exists in various forms, but it is highlighted by the ongoing ideological struggle between Skinner and Carl Rogers, the firmly humanistic founder of client-centered therapy, advocate of encounter groups, and developer of person-centered theory. Rogers's work has been well known in psychology since the 1940s, and he is widely respected for his contributions. Rogers's humanism predated the use of the label "humanistic psychology," but he now identifies himself with that broad school of thought.

Skinner and Rogers have brought a clear focus to the differences between radical behaviorism and the humanistic approach. They have met in public debates and frequently mention each other in their writings. Their opposition to each other's ideas has been healthy and constructive, bringing out important issues for consideration. Each seems to like the other personally. Skinner has pointed out that he doesn't generally engage in arguments or debates, being much more interested in simply presenting his own views, but says that he has made an exception in the case of his friend, Carl Rogers. Rogers, despite sharp differences with his ideas, has expressed respect for Skinner's honesty and dedication to his work.

After briefly presenting some of the major aspects of Rogers's humanistic approach, which has strongly influenced many humanistic psychologists, we will consider the specifics of the controversy between him and Skinner.

ROGERS'S HUMANISTIC APPROACH

Rogers believes that human nature is essentially positive: basically we seek growth and fulfillment (actualization) and we want close and meaningful relations with others. He suggests that in order for actualization to occur and for interpersonal relations to be positive and fulfilling, we must be accurately aware of our basic inner experiencing (sensations, perceptions, feelings, thoughts, etc.).

Why do so many people fail to actualize themselves? What goes wrong? Rogers explains that we have a need for *positive regard* (love and acceptance) from significant other persons in our lives and we often receive *conditional*, rather than *unconditional*, positive regard. This means that conditions (or stipulations) are placed on the love and acceptance that we need. In simple terms, the message often received is "I will love and accept you *if* you believe or feel as I expect you to." When we get such messages directly or subtly, we are apt to yield in varying degrees to receive the positive regard that we crave—even when it means giving up what our own inner experiencing is telling us. We may deny, distort, and defend against this experiencing and convince ourselves, for example, that our sexual feelings are bad, that our occasional anger toward our parents is wrong, that creative interests must come second to "serious" pursuits, and so on. In our attempts to defend against the aspects of our inner experiencing that are considered "bad" or "wrong", (and to prevent rejection by significant others, especially during our formative years) we become more rigid, less aware of basic feelings, and less spontaneous. Our self-concepts become distorted in the direction of others' standards and values, rather than being closely related to our own deeply felt inner experiencing. In brief, this is Rogers's explanation of how we become derailed from the track toward actualization.

If we are to develop in actualizing ways, Rogers suggests that *unconditional positive regard* is important. That is, we need love and acceptance without conditions (or stipulations) being placed on them.[1] We then can remain in tune with our basic experiencing, accepting and responding to our own personal inner reactions in an open way, developing as flexible, aware, spontaneous, nondefensive persons, and tending toward behaviors that are beneficial to ourselves and society. We can sense what our own real fundamental needs and wants are, while also being aware of what the surrounding environmental circumstances require. To understand Rogers's thinking, it is necessary to remember that he has an optimistic view of human nature. He is saying that if persons are allowed to develop in a warm, accepting atmosphere, they will not only actualize themselves, but will live and work more harmoniously with others.

In *client-centered psychotherapy*, which Rogers developed, the therapist attempts to create interpersonal conditions that will allow clients to regain contact with their basic inner experiencing. The three major attitudes that client-centered therapists try to maximize are: (1) *empathic understanding*, (2) *unconditional positive regard*, and (3) *genuineness*. If the therapist can sense empathically the subjective meanings that experiences have for

---

[1] The concept of *unconditional positive regard* is different from Skinner's concept of *positive reinforcement*. The idea behind unconditional positive regard is that if a person is completely accepted for what he or she is, the person will develop in positive ways; again, Rogers's positive view of basic human nature is important if this concept is to be assumed workable. Skinner makes no assumptions about human nature being either positive or negative; therefore he suggests that positive reinforcement be used to shape and maintain desirable and constructive behaviors.

the client, and reflect this understanding, the client can gain clearer perspectives on these experiences. By accepting and caring for the client unconditionally, the therapist presumably helps the client to become more self-accepting and to allow a fuller range of thoughts, feelings, perceptions, and sensations into awareness without self-condemnation. By being genuine or "real," the therapist maintains an honest interaction with the client, dropping the pretenses and false facades that often prevail in everyday life. If these three therapist attitudes—empathy, unconditional positive regard, and genuineness—can be maintained with reasonable consistency, Rogers believes that clients will grasp the essential meanings of their own inner experiencing and beneficial behavioral changes will result.

In Rogers's view, each of us has within us the resources to actualize our true selves, and these resources are mobilized if adequate conditions are provided. Client-centered therapists claim considerable success with their clients. Despite these successes, however, there is not sufficient evidence to state conclusively that Rogers's *interpretation* of why clients improve during therapy is correct.

THE ROGERS-SKINNER CONTROVERSY

Skinner has been critical of Rogers's assumptions about what occurs during therapy. Client-centered therapy emphasizes the client's responsibility for getting better. Though the therapist sets the conditions of empathy, unconditional positive regard, and genuineness, it is the client who must get in touch with inner experiencing and choose how to live. Skinner suggests that the notions of the client looking within, and making free choices about what to do, are irrelevant. In his view, there are no answers deep within the person. People are always controlled in one way or another and the goal should be to free them from *aversive* control. They often need assistance in developing different, more effective behaviors and in finding new sources of positive reinforcement, but there is no such thing as free choice based on inner experiencing. According to Skinner, free choice is an illusion.

Skinner implies that client-centered therapists *do* control patients in subtle ways, despite denials of such control. With subtle verbal statements and physical gestures (for example, nodding the head at particular times), client-centered therapists may inadvertently shape certain behaviors in their clients. Skinner indicates that if a client-centered therapist actually is successful in maintaining a completely nonjudgmental stance, the client then will be controlled by forces outside of the therapy situation, such as the reactions of others and earlier religious or ethical training. The effects of these outside influences may change because of aspects of the therapy experience; for example, the client may become more assertive with others because he or she is being encouraged subtly by the therapist to talk about feelings and to "be honest." In Skinner's view, any changes that occur in the client's behaviors are due to such environmental experiences and *not* to changes in inner states such as the self-concept.

Skinner's thoroughgoing emphasis on objective behavioral determinants, and Rogers's persistent belief that inner, subjective experiencing is basic and essential, form the basis of other disagreements between the two psychologists. Rogers has suggested that in addition to the objective research of the behaviorists it is important to try to grasp subjectively what persons are experiencing within. This is a *phenomenological approach*. He believes that an important influence on individuals is their immediate, conscious experiencing of themselves and the world around them, and that if persons are to be understood fully we must be able to view reality through their eyes. In short, a person's subjective view of reality is important in determining how he or she will act. For example, the same barking dog may affect two people differently because of their different subjective perceptions of the situation. One person may walk over and pet the dog, while the other person runs away. In Rogers's view, if we are to understand these two different reactions, we must understand how each person perceives the barking dog.

Skinner reacts to such suggestions by pointing out that we can't gain direct knowledge of another person's inner experiencing. We don't have immediate access to these inner processes, and Skinner believes that it is futile to try to build scientific knowledge on inferences about subjective states. Rather, we must stick to objective approaches and look for functional relationships between observable events and observable behaviors. For example, in the preceding case, there is no reason to assume that the two persons react differently to a barking dog because of different "subjective perceptions." A Skinnerian analysis suggests that they have had different experiences with dogs. These experiences, reinforcing or punishing, can be considered the critical factors determining approach or avoidance behaviors. Skinner believes that by considering internal states (such as "subjective perceptions") as causes of behavior, the environmental determinants tend to be underemphasized or overlooked (Skinner similarly has criticized Freud's speculations about inner states—see chapter 6).

Another difference of opinion between Rogers and Skinner involves educational practices. Rogers believes that learning should occur in a relatively unstructured setting, in which resources are available to the learner so that he or she can pursue personal interests. In his view, people are naturally curious and if they are free to follow their own chosen paths of learning they will educate themselves. He feels that self-guided learning should be the crux of education. The schools should trust students to follow their own leads and allow for emotional, as well as intellectual, learning. He refers to this as educating the "whole person."

It is interesting that both Rogers and Skinner are very critical of the existing educational system and recommend drastic changes. Rogers advocates less structure and more freedom for students—education should be student-centered. On the other side, Skinner advocates *more* structure, but of a different type than now exists. He is strongly opposed to the use of aversive control to promote learning. He believes that too often students are exposed to threats of punishment (poor grades, reprimands, failure, etc.) as a means of getting them to work hard. In his view, education should be based on positive reinforcement. Students should be given material in sufficiently small units so that each unit can be mastered. The student's progress can therefore be reinforced before the next unit is undertaken. In this way, effective learning takes place and the student's feelings about the experience are positive (Skinner says that positive reinforcement results in good feelings). To say that Skinner advocates a more structured education means that he favors carefully planned, systematic presentations of material with ample opportunities for the learner's progress to be reinforced (programmed material and teaching machines are helpful in this regard).

Skinner suggests that his educational goals are in agreement with those of Rogers: They both want people to feel positively about their educational experiences and to develop independence. (Also, they both are very optimistic about the potential of humans to learn, given adequate conditions.) By "independence" he means that persons should be able to act without having to be told what to do and when to do it. Also, he wants people to *feel* free even though they actually can never *be* free from the effects of environmental factors. To Skinner, independence and feelings of freedom come from building a rich repertoire of behaviors based on positive reinforcement, and from situations in which aversive control is absent. He believes that Rogers' reliance on inner determinants to motivate and guide learning is misplaced, and suggests that "motivation" and "inner guidance" do not emerge from somewhere within the person. Rather, behaviors that indicate these qualities result from appropriate reinforcements.

The suggestions of both Rogers and Skinner have been applied in various educational settings with claims of considerable success. Who, then, is right? At this point there is no conclusive answer. There are so many different types of subject matter, student abilities and backgrounds, educational situations, and other relevant factors, that it is premature to judge one approach as being the most effective overall. Also, there may be certain common elements of learning situations that produce good outcomes. For example, when Skinner's systematic, structured approach is used, a certain amount of general "warmth and acceptance" on the part of the instructor may be important (Skinner would probably agree with this, but would add that "warmth and acceptance" should be defined in terms of specific instructor behaviors). When Rogers's approach is used, it is likely that certain basic skills can be taught most efficiently with a systematic approach, before allowing students "to pursue their own interests" (Rogers would probably agree with this, but would add that it is always important that students *want* to learn the material, however basic it is). In short, it doesn't seem that the two approaches are necessarily mutually exclusive. However, the larger behaviorist-humanist educational dispute focuses on the issue of the importance of outer versus inner determinants of learning.

Rogers's belief that human nature essentially is positive ties in with his educational beliefs. He feels that there are growth potentials within each person that need to be released. Skinner, on the other hand, suggests that the positive forces assumed to lie deep within our personalities are simply the things that we can accomplish with appropriate reinforcement. These different perspectives on human nature affect educational perspectives. For Rogers, freedom to develop inner resources is foremost, which leads to "open classrooms" and other unstructured settings. For Skinner, the planning of environmental conditions is foremost, which leads to systematic applications of positive reinforcement in the classroom and to the use of programmed material and teaching machines.

At a 1956 symposium featuring an exchange between Rogers and Skinner, Rogers indicated that he believes "the major flaw" in the type of behavioral control advocated by Skinner "is the denial, misunderstanding, or gross underestimation of the place of ends, goals or values in their relationship to science."[2] This comment

[2] Carl Rogers and B. F. Skinner, "Some Issues Concerning the Control of Human Behavior," *Science*, 124, no. 3231 (November 30, 1956), p. 1061.

brings out yet another aspect of the controversy between these two men. Rogers went on to explain that there is always a "prior subjective choice" about the purposes of scientific work, once again pointing out what he considers an essential part of all human pursuits: inner subjective experiencing. In his opinion, even the most objective behavioral scientist must make certain value decisions that are outside of science itself. In other words, the scientist must decide what to study, how to study it, and how to use the data obtained, and these decisions arise from the inner experiencing of the scientist. For Rogers, the initial decision to be objective and scientific cannot itself be derived from science; rather, it is a subjectively chosen value.

In response to Rogers's statements about the significance of subjective value choices, Skinner indicates that these choices are really determined by reinforcement. Some behavioral outcomes are reinforcing and others aren't. People "choose" or "decide" to do that which is reinforcing. Expanding on Skinner's reasoning, it can be said that the scientist's behaviors, and accompanying "values," are also controlled by reinforcements, rather than by some inner choice that he or she makes to engage in scientific pursuits. If the background of a scientist were known in detail, it would very likely show a shaping process that led the scientist to use certain techniques and to study certain phenomena. Simply stated, scientists do what they do (and hold certain scientific values) because their science-related behaviors have been reinforced, perhaps by parents and teachers initially, and later by their colleagues. Also, the fact that an experiment produces results may be reinforcing in and of itself. (Skinner has suggested that his own productive scientific career has been influenced by a fortunate personal history of reinforcement for such efforts.) Considering the possible influences of reinforcers on the scientist's behavior, is it still necessary to say that he or she "chooses" to do research? The answer to this question depends on whether you are a humanist or a behaviorist. The humanist insists that choice enters into the process, while the behaviorist maintains that the notion of choice is irrelevant.

To conclude this section, let's briefly consider the differences between Rogers and Skinner on the issue of broad social change. Rogers's writings indicate that he favors an opening up of society's institutions, in the sense that they should be more responsive to innovations and more geared toward change based on the needs of individuals for growth and fulfillment. He feels that society essentially is too static. Rigid rules and codes of expected conduct stifle the creative development of mature, actualized individuals. Rogers perhaps has been most vocal about the restricting influences of two of our most revered social institutions: education and the family. He feels that they exert too much inhibiting control over persons and need to change in the direction of fostering freedom and actualization.

The most basic difference between Rogers's and Skinner's views on society involves the issue of control. Rogers believes that we need much less of it. Skinner believes that we must have it, but in a different form than exists presently. Skinner indicates that behavioral engineering—the systematic application of behavioral techniques—is essential for an effective society. The type of control that Skinner recommends is based on positive reinforcement. People should behave in productive and creative ways because society positively reinforces such behaviors. In other words, the present extensive use of punishment and aversive control by social institutions must be replaced by positive forms of control. This is the general formula offered by Skinner for social change (other recommendations will be discussed in chapter 8). Both he and Rogers are equally adamant about the need for social change, but they differ on the question of how to bring about the desired outcomes.

It is interesting to consider what makes a person a humanist or a behaviorist. Rogers would say that it is mainly a matter of choice, while Skinner would say that it depends strongly on the individual's history of reinforcement. Basically, this implies that Rogers (from his perspective) has made a subjective decision to be a humanist, while Skinner (from his perspective) has been conditioned by environmental factors to be behavioristic. Regardless of the determining factors, humanists and behaviorists differ in the terminology they use to describe and explain human functioning, in the kinds of research they do, in their therapeutic techniques, in their educational procedures, and in their prescriptions for social change. The humanist-behaviorist controversy isn't likely to subside quickly. The issues involved are significant and complex, and very difficult (perhaps even impossible) to resolve completely.

EIGHT

IS SKINNERIAN PSYCHOLOGY RELEVANT FOR TODAY'S WORLD?

Skinner has addressed contemporary social problems in a number of ways. As indicated in the preceding chapter, he has suggested changes in our educational system and in other social institutions. His novel, *Walden Two*, shows how behavioral concepts might be applied in a small community, and his more recent book, *Beyond Freedom and Dignity*, deals with the broad question of the survival of the culture and society's need for behavioral technology. Also, he has written articles and given lectures on these topics. With regard to practical applications of Skinner's behavioral procedures, many therapists, psychologists, teachers, business and industrial supervisors, parents, and others, have used them effectively in a variety of real-life situations.

Judging from all this activity, the answer to the question in the chapter heading would seem to be an unqualified "Yes." Though there are many persons, including Carl Rogers and other humanistic psychologists, who have strong reservations about the widespread use of Skinner's concepts and techniques, there is little doubt that their use is increasing. That fact alone is evidence that Skinnerian psychology *is* relevant, that it does pertain to various situations in today's world.

In this chapter we'll discuss some of Skinner's general concerns about our society and its directions. However, we won't cover the specific procedures that constitute the growing field of "behavior modification," which involves practical applications of the behavioral concepts of Skinner and others. There are publications that treat the specifics of current work in that field, and these should be consulted by those who are interested.[1]

---

[1] There are many relevant books and articles. To name a few of the books: Garry Martin and Joseph Pear, *Behavior Modification: What It Is and How to Do It*

When Skinner wrote *Walden Two* in 1945 (it was published three years later), he was attempting to show the possibilities of applying behavioral concepts derived from laboratory research to the running of a small community. (He estimated the size of the town as one thousand but has indicated that the best number might be different; the most effective size needs to be determined through experimentation.) The book sold slowly for a number of years, but then began an upward trend that has reached over one million copies.

Skinner says that when he wrote *Walden Two* he was guessing how his experimental results could be applied. At that time, nothing actually had been done to test these findings in practical human situations. Today, however, he believes that much less guessing is necessary. The tremendous growth in the behavior-modification movement, especially during the 1960s and since, has provided evidence that human behavior can be affected beneficially by applying laboratory-derived procedures. This has been shown in "normal" situations such as public schools and businesses, as well as in institutions that care for retardates, psychotics, and other persons with special problems. This evidence allows greater confidence in the possibilities for planned communities based on behavioral technology.

Although there have been no experimental communities that have followed exactly the fictional *Walden Two*, the general model

(Englewood Cliffs, N. J.: Prentice-Hall, Inc., 1978); Ellen P. Reese, *Human Behavior: Analysis and Application*, 2nd ed. (Dubuque, Iowa: Wm. C. Brown Company Publishers, 1978); Judith Elbert Favell, *The Power of Positive Reinforcement: A Handbook of Behavior Modification* (Springfield, Ill.: Charles C. Thomas, Publisher, 1977); W. Edward Craighead, Alan E. Kazdin, and Michael J. Mahoney, *Behavior Modification: Principles, Issues, and Applications* (Boston: Houghton Mifflin Company, 1976); William Redd and William Sleator, *Take Charge: A Comprehensive Analysis of Behavior Modification* (New York: Vintage Books, 1976); and Roger Ulrich, Thomas Stachnik, and John Mabry, eds., *Control of Human Behavior*, Vol. 2 (Glenview, Ill.: Scott, Foresman and Company, 1970). The *Journal of Applied Behavior Analysis* is devoted to articles on practical applications of behavioral techniques and is a primary source of information for interested persons.

provided by Skinner has been used. The oldest example is Twin Oaks, near Louisa, Virginia. It was begun in 1967 by eight people and has evolved over the years as the membership and community practices have changed. Kathleen Kinkade, one of the original members, wrote a book describing the community (*A Walden Two Experiment: The First Five Years of Twin Oaks Community*, published by William Morrow and Company, 1973). In a foreword to this book, Skinner points out that even though the development of Twin Oaks has not been identical to what he proposed in *Walden Two*, it is a valuable test of the application of certain fundamental ideas and provides interesting information. He believes that experimental communities have to cope with problems that are similar to those the world is facing. Therefore, the outcomes of these attempts are relevant to larger issues.

Some of Skinner's suggestions about important aspects of community life, as expressed in *Walden Two* and other writings, are as follows: (1) *child rearing* should be communal, so that the security and training of children doesn't depend solely on the presence and abilities of biological parents; specialists should have primary responsibility for the day-to-day care of children, thereby preventing problems caused by inexperience, inconsistent demands, abuse, overprotection, and other shortcomings of modern family life; (2) *education* should be related to practical situations within the community, so that students see concrete applications of the subject matter; additional provisions, such as specialized books and other materials, should be made for those who want to pursue particular interests; programmed materials and teaching machines should be used more extensively; (3) *work* should be productive, with everyone expected to contribute a modest amount of effort; the emphasis within the community should be on a simple, but satisfying, life; there should be no need for long hours of work to provide useless services or goods; (4) *leisure time* should be ample, and activities should center on doing rather than merely observing; (5) *personal relations* should be noncompetitive and intimate, making it more likely that people will be friendly and affectionate toward each other; intimacy among community members also is important because it allows immediate approval of desirable behaviors and censure of undesirable behaviors; in other words, the impersonal situations that characterize much of contemporary society should be avoided; (6) *sex roles* should not be structured along traditional lines, but rather both men and women should pursue whatever work or leisure activities that fit their abilities; child-rearing should not be solely the women's responsibility; (7) *young people and old people* should have active roles in community life; the young should be allowed to assume a full role earlier, including work and marriage, and the old should be able to contribute longer; (8) *psychotics, retardates, and others with special problems* should be cared for within the community, and some useful role should be found for them whenever possible; behavior-modification procedures are often effective with these persons, allowing them to perform useful tasks and to enjoy certain leisure activities; (9) *government* operates best when people behave responsibly toward one another; in fact, when people in a community have a face-to-face familiarity with each other, and interact in cooperative and reinforcing ways, there is very little need for governmental regulations.

In order to accomplish the above, Skinner suggests that "smaller would be better" with regard to our living circumstances. It is easier to apply behavioral procedures in small communities than in major population areas or in large, complex organizations. Small communities provide the advantages of close interpersonal contacts. Also, if important reinforcers (productive work, contacts with friends, leisure activities, etc.) are available *within* the community, there is less need for traveling and therefore less wasted time and resources. In short, Skinner believes that it would be more efficient, and easier to plan and manage things, if people were decentralized and lived in small towns. He sees a network of Walden-Two type communities as a constructive alternative to our present system.

An essential feature of the small communities visualized by Skinner is that they be "experimental." This means that the results of each social change should be monitored closely to see that they are beneficial to individuals and to the community. This approach is similar to that used in scientific laboratories, where the researcher varies some factor in order to study its effects. This method of systematically instituting changes, and carefully checking the results, allows corrections to be made before undesirable outcomes multiply. Again, it is a matter of paying attention to the consequences of actions, something that Skinner emphasizes consistently. In his opinion, we do far too little of it. We often make changes and *assume* that certain outcomes occur, without collecting data or making careful observations to back up our assumptions. If Skinner's advice were followed, we would behave more like scientists when planning and managing our lives and the communities within which we live.

Fundamentally, what Skinner advocates is a cultural revolution. He believes that major changes must be made in our overcrowded, overconsuming, and impersonal society. Our survival, he suggests, may well depend on these changes. His answer to our social problems doesn't rely on political action or governmental regulations. Rather, what is needed is the application of behavioral-science findings to our everyday lives, and the acquisition of more knowledge about the effects of environmental conditions on behavior.

BEYOND FREEDOM AND DIGNITY

Skinner's 1971 book, *Beyond Freedom and Dignity*, expresses themes similar to some of those in *Walden Two*. However, it isn't a work of fiction; rather, it is a treatise on the need for behavioral technology (or behavioral engineering) in today's society and the problems involved in establishing such a technology. In earlier chapters, we covered a number of points that are related to Skinner's ideas in *Beyond Freedom and Dignity*, but now we'll look directly at several major issues discussed in that book. Again, I'll try to present Skinner's ideas as simply as possible and will provide some of my own elaborations and examples. For fuller details on his views, *Beyond Freedom and Dignity* should be consulted.

Skinner suggests that though enormous advances have been made in fields such as biology and physics, allowing sophisticated technologies to be developed with regard to contraception, weapons' systems, agriculture, medicine, and so on, there has been relatively little progress in the development of a technology of behavior. A science of human behavior upon which such a technology could be based has been slow to emerge, and therefore governmental, educational, economic, and other social institutions continue to plod along, showing little improvement over the years.

As mentioned at the beginning of this chapter, recent years have seen a growing use of behavior-modification techniques based on the principles of Skinner and his colleagues, and this represents progress in the development and application of behavioral technology. However, despite this trend, Skinner believes that there exists widespread resistance to advances in this type of approach to individual and social problems. This resistance may prevent us from moving with sufficient speed toward the broader development and use of a technology of behavior, and our society may suffer severely from ever-increasing difficulties as a result. He expresses considerable doubt about our continued ability to maintain a viable and strong society unless we take more seriously the role of a science of human behavior.

Why is it that while other sciences have shown dramatic progress, behavioral science has lagged behind? Skinner indicates that the major reason is that we look for the causes of behavior in the wrong place. We tend to look for internal causes, residing within individuals: intentions, purposes, decisions, aims, values, plans, and so on, commonly are considered the moving forces behind our actions. Feelings and states of mind are emphasized in explaining why people behave as they do. We give relatively little attention to either antecedent or existing environmental conditions, and Skinner believes that it is these conditions that provide the details upon which a science of behavior must be built.

Why do we continue to insist on inner motivators of behavior, rather than taking a more thorough look at environmental causes? Two important reasons suggested by Skinner are: (1) since we do have feelings, often strong and immediate ones, they seem to us to cause our behaviors, and (2) environmental influences on behavior often are subtle and difficult to observe, and therefore easily go unnoticed.

It is easy to understand why feelings seem to cause behavior. They exist immediately within us, are many times intense, and they accompany our actions. It would be surprising if we *didn't* believe they caused our behaviors. In Skinner's view, however, they are "by-products" of the same environmental conditions that influence how we behave. To give a couple of simple examples (similar to ones given earlier in this book), if you are reinforced with praise or approval for something you do, you not only are more likely to do it again, but you also are likely to "feel good." In other words, reinforcement has affected both your behavior *and* your feelings. In another case, you might be punished for something you do. You then would not be likely to repeat it immediately, and you would probably feel guilt, resentment, anger, or some other emotion, depending on the circumstances. The important point made by Skinner is that "feeling good" or "feeling guilty" is not what causes your behaviors. These feelings are controlled by environmental factors such as reinforcements and punishments, just as overt behaviors are controlled by these consequences.

Environmental influences on behavior often aren't obvious and therefore don't provide a clear alternative explanation. The effects of the environment are often misunderstood. Skinner explains that the environment doesn't primarily push or pull us around; rather, it *selects* certain behaviors because of their consequences. A behavior is *selected* (becomes more likely to occur) if it is reinforced. We emit many different types of responses during our lifetimes, but only some of them become part of our regular behavior patterns. Those that do are the ones that have reinforcing consequences (they are either *positively* or *negatively* reinforced—see chapter 3 for more details). The selective nature of the environment often operates inconspicuously; it doesn't "stand out" with dramatic force as do our feelings. Therefore, much of the determining action of the environment (including both physical and social factors) goes unnoticed, while we focus on the more obvious feelings that we have or that others express. (Skinner draws a parallel between Darwin's theory of evolution and his own ideas. Evolutionary theory emphasizes the selective nature of the environment with regard to *genetic* characteristics, and Skinner emphasizes the selective nature of the environment with regard to *behavioral* characteristics.)

The results of realizing that the environment *selects* behaviors because of their consequences are: (1) explanations based on feelings and other inner states of mind are abandoned in favor of the careful examination of environmental factors; and (2) desirable behavioral changes are brought about by changing the environmental conditions to which persons are exposed. Skinner points out that he and his colleagues have been proceeding along these lines, and in recent years great advances have been made in developing a technology of behavior. What stands in the way of greater use of this technology are certain traditional ideas that are prevalent in our society and pervade our legal, economic, and educational systems, as well as other social institutions.

The ideas that are especially opposed to the development and use of behavioral technology have to do with individual autonomy: the *freedom* of each person to choose or decide his or her own course of action and the *dignity* (or worth) that is awarded the person who successfully overcomes obstacles or achieves admirable goals. The controversy that arises from challenges to freedom and dignity gets in the way of an objective appraisal of the benefits of a technology of behavior.

The title of his book, *Beyond Freedom and Dignity*, indicates the central issue that Skinner believes is involved in the adoption of a behavioral-technology approach to solving society's problems. He suggests that we must move *beyond* the traditional concepts of *freedom and dignity* and stop acting in terms of individual autonomy. We must investigate and develop environmental conditions that will reduce overpopulation, disease, pollution, and other social ills, while promoting health, peace, conservation of natural resources, and other socially beneficial goals. As long as people are seen as autonomous beings who have the *freedom* to decide their own fates and whose *dignity* or worth depends on admirable actions arising from their personal inner qualities, we will not focus sufficiently on the controlling influences of the environment. Therefore, we will miss opportunities to develop a stronger and better society by improving the conditions that affect our behaviors.

In discussing the details of "freedom," Skinner suggests that commonly it is seen as a state of mind or a feeling, and that humans generally are considered to have a will to be free. Therefore, there is an emphasis on the need to throw off aversive control so that the individual can be free to live life on his or her own terms. Unfortunately, this line of reasoning easily leads to the conclusion that all control is wrong, and the possibility of controlling social conditions for beneficial results tends to be either ignored or actively rejected. In Skinner's view, we not only should try to free persons from aversive control (which is what the advocates of freedom recommend), but we should take the next step and create controls which produce positive outcomes. If we remain fixed on the notion that "freedom" is threatened by *all* forms of control, we lose the advantages that behavioral technology can provide.

The traditional concept of "dignity," which involves worthiness bestowed on individuals when they are given credit for admirable behaviors, also is threatened by behavioral technology. In Skinner's approach, all behavior is determined by genetic and environmental factors, and there are no "admirable behaviors" arising out of the depths of one's special "inner character" or "personality." In other words, what we do (admirable or not) is viewed by Skinner as the result of conditions (genetic and environmental) that we have no part in "deciding upon" or "choosing;" therefore, credit-giving is inappropriate when it implies that the person has acted autonomously. We are so used to giving credit to, and honoring, individuals for their achievements, and to seeking credit and honor for ourselves, that Skinner's suggestions are likely to seem alien to us.

In cases when credit is given or taken for accomplishments, the causes of these accomplishments are not readily observable. There are many examples of heroic, artistic, inventive, persevering, and other "admirable" behaviors in which the only available explanation seems to be that there is some special inner quality of the hero, the artist, the inventor, or the hard-working individual. Behavioral science, as advocated by Skinner, involves the examination of how these types of behaviors (as well as "ordinary" behaviors) come about through environmental influences. His assumption is that environmental circumstances, however subtle or inconspicuous, *are* influential. Once the relevant environmental conditions are discovered, this knowledge can then be used to promote further socially beneficial accomplishments. A problem emerges, however, when we balk at this approach because it seems to reduce our dignity.

Skinner suggests that we don't really want to discover the external circumstances that control our "admirable" behaviors because we no longer would be able to "take credit" for them—our "worth," *as we presently conceive it*, would be reduced. This situation blocks the maximum development and use of environmental controls that could lead to greater human accomplishments.

In *Beyond Freedom and Dignity*, Skinner takes up another issue that he has discussed in many other publications, including *Walden Two:* the role of punishment in society. He again points out that we frequently control and are controlled by punitive means, such as actual or threatened censure, ridicule, criticism, or physical harm. Social institutions such as those of government and religion, as well as individuals, often use punishment (or threatened punishment) as a way of suppressing unwanted behaviors.

Though punishment tends to be effective on an immediate

basis, and may continue to suppress behavior if the punisher remains present (or if it was of sufficient intensity), Skinner indicates that it fails in the long run. It doesn't eliminate tendencies to behave in punishable ways; the punished person will still "want to do" what he or she has been punished for. Also, as was mentioned earlier in this book, the use of punishment may result in escape or avoidance behaviors. Individuals who are punished or threatened with punishment are likely to find ways of getting away from the punishing circumstances: School children may cut classes, workers may quit or feign illnesses, wives or husbands may desert their spouses, and so on.

Another good example of what Skinner is talking about are laws that rely on punitive measures and aversive control for their effectiveness. Speed limits, for example, are maintained primarily by the tickets given to those who speed, by the threat of receiving a ticket, by the presence of police, or by indications that speed-monitoring equipment is being used. In the absence of these conditions, many individuals exceed the speed limit. Also, in order to avoid the punishment of receiving a ticket, drivers use various techniques such as radar detectors.

Following Skinner's approach, perhaps another system for maintaining speed limits should be introduced which provides positive reinforcement for slower driving. It might sound far-fetched, but maybe the main purpose of highway police should be to notice good driving and to signal their approval (instead of the reprimand or speeding ticket that usually follows being noticed by the police). Additionally, letters of praise could be sent (although the effectiveness of this reinforcer might be limited because it is not immediate; reinforcers are most effective when they immediately follow the appropriate behavior). Another possibility would be to put gas-mileage markings on the speedometer, so that driving at reasonable speeds would be reinforced immediately by the indication that good gas mileage was being obtained.

Returning to Skinner's views on punishment, he suggests that it is possible to construct a society in which punishable behaviors occur infrequently or never. In other words, if behavioral technology were used to control behavior in nonpunitive ways, good behaviors would be common and there would be little need for punitive techniques. This suggestion, Skinner indicates, is not easily accepted by those who advocate freedom of choice and who accept the traditional concept of human dignity based on individual, autonomous control of one's own achievements. In simple terms, the objections are that if a person's good behavior is determined by environmental control, what happens to his or her freedom to choose to be good, and how can credit be given for behaving well?

Again, the idea of individual autonomy enters the picture, and actually supports (in an indirect way) the retention of punitive measures. In a punitive society, if persons are good it seems to be because they have chosen to be good and therefore they deserve credit. It's like saying: "If you don't take personal responsibility for yourself and don't control yourself in the appropriate ways, you will be punished. You have the choice. It's up to you. If you decide to behave well, you will be showing strong character and you will deserve to be admired." Skinner believes that this is a relatively ineffective way to get people to behave well (as is obvious just by looking at all of the undesirable behaviors that exist). However, it does allow the advocates of freedom and dignity to feel comfortable, because individuals appear to have the freedom to decide whether or not they will do the correct thing and credit can then be given to those who "make the proper decisions." If an effective and nonpunitive behavioral technology were introduced, and people behaved well because of planned environmental conditions, there would be no "personal responsibility" for good behavior, no "freedom" to choose to behave well, and no "dignity" bestowed on individuals for their achievements.

Of course, that doesn't mean that *feelings* of responsibility, freedom, and dignity would be eliminated. It simply means that the traditional reliance upon these concepts, which now dominate society, would be replaced with behavioral-technology procedures. As Skinner has pointed out time and again, the basic approach of his behavioral technology is positive reinforcement. This is his preferred means of controlling behavior, and it not only is effective in getting people to behave well: it also makes them feel good.

Skinner himself believes that his own behavior is controlled primarily by his environment. He doesn't see himself as an exception to the rules of his psychology. Despite the fact that he is controlled by environmental conditions (for example, the reinforcing consequences of his research and writing behaviors) he says that he feels free. This feeling of freedom does not depend on *actually* being free (Skinner says there is no such thing): It comes from a positively reinforcing environment. So, in a Skinnerian society using behavioral technology, people would still be able to feel free, worthy, and responsible, even though their behaviors were being controlled. (An important point: Skinner believes that we *presently* are controlled by our environments and that there is no way to escape being controlled; the goal then, in his view, is to construct nonpunitive and maximally effective environmental conditions that will promote individual and social improvements—and good feelings.)

In a society that relies heavily on punitive techniques to control individuals, much time and effort is wasted as people attempt to escape or avoid punishing consequences (and, of course, these punitive techniques also produce negative feelings in those being controlled). This weakens the society; a stronger society is likely when positive reinforcement is used systematically to shape and maintain productive and beneficial activities.

In our society, despite the high incidence of punitive control, there obviously are numerous successful persons who develop their potential and contribute to society. But should we be satisfied with this? Also, are there countertrends, such as delinquency, crime, unemployment, pollution, and wasted resources, that need correcting before they bring the downfall of society? Skinner's behavioral-technology suggestions are directed at improving the functioning of society through a more systematic and scientifically based approach. In other words, his plan leaves less to chance. Though some fortunate individuals presently are exposed to favorable environmental conditions, Skinner raises the possibility of making such exposure more common. If he is correct, and if his plan were adopted on a wide scale, it would mobilize human potential far beyond present hopes.

In addressing the issue of whether or not our culture will survive in the long run, Skinner points out the importance of inducing individuals to work for its survival. Expressing a familiar theme, he suggests that we can't rely on wise judgments, feelings of concern, or other mental or emotional states to save us. Rather, positive thoughts, enthusiastic feelings, *and* (most importantly) culture-saving behaviors, all depend on the ways in which the culture provides positive and negative reinforcers, and the emphasis is best placed on positive reinforcement.

In *Walden Two*, Skinner presents his ideas for a utopian society based on behavioral-science findings. It is a fictional community, in which child-rearing, work, leisure, and other important human activities are controlled beneficially by the manipulation of environmental conditions. In *Beyond Freedom and Dignity*, Skinner's main point is that the traditional values of freedom and dignity, which emphasize doing away with all forms of external control, prevent the maximum development of behavioral science and the use of behavioral technology. The advocates of freedom and dignity, in his view, have been so involved in suppressing punitive controlling techniques that they fail to see the benefits of constructive environmental control. According to Skinner, it is a fact that all of us are controlled all of the time. Therefore, it would be better if we designed positive controls to replace those that are aversive or punitive, and to shape behaviors that would help insure the survival of our culture.

The points mentioned in this chapter do not cover all that Skinner has said about contemporary society, but some highlights have been presented. In both *Walden Two* and *Beyond Freedom and Dignity*, as well as in other writings, he has discussed other issues that are too involved to go into here. Some of these issues are quite subtle and require careful study to be understood fully.

NINE

PERSONAL
REFLECTIONS

In this chapter, I'll discuss Skinnerian psychology in more personal terms, indicating what I believe to be some of the most important influences that it can have in our everyday lives. More of my own views are presented than in previous chapters. Actually, of course, this whole book reflects my perspectives on Skinner. Throughout, I've selected and emphasized certain portions of his writings, using examples and making interpretations that I believe clarify his work. While doing this, I've tried to convey his ideas without altering their essential content. In this chapter, I'll continue in that general vein. However, while still trying to interpret Skinner accurately, I'll put more emphasis on how I personally view the applications of his approach.

Being positively affected by Skinner's concepts can occur very dramatically (that is, a person can become a thoroughgoing radical behaviorist) or it can occur with varying degrees of less intense acceptance. It seems, though, judging from discussions I've had with a wide range of individuals, that in many cases persons tend to reject everything he says simply because they disagree with certain aspects of his approach. To the extent that this is true, it's unfortunate. His suggestions cover a wide variety of important issues and ways of looking at the behaviors of ourselves and others, and they can be useful even when they aren't accepted totally. In other words, there's no need to discard the whole approach even if parts of it are found objectionable.

As I indicated in the first chapter, I find much of what Skinner says to be very reasonable and useful, although I'm not sure that all the answers to life's situations and problems are to be found in radical behaviorism. I continue trying to apply it and to test out its assumptions in everyday life. So far, it has proved to be a very satisfactory way of explaining (to me) much of what goes on in my own life, in the lives of others, and in society at large. (Perhaps I should point out that I don't walk around all day thinking, "What would Skinner say about this?" or "What would Skinner do in this situation?" Rather, I simply try to think in behavioristic terms when some behavior—my own or someone else's—or some situation, needs explaining. Also, I try to apply some behavioristic concepts to myself and to my interactions with others.)

POSITIVE REINFORCEMENT
IN INTERPERSONAL RELATIONS

A fundamental concept of Skinnerian psychology is positive reinforcement: Behaviors are strengthened if they are followed by certain stimuli (which are called positive reinforcers). Many of the important positive reinforcers in everyday life—attention, approval, appreciation, and affection—are given and received through social interactions. Not only does positive reinforcement strengthen behavior, but often it causes the recipient to have "good feelings." These facts have been pointed out repeatedly in previous chapters, but perhaps it will pay to look at positive reinforcement one more time. It's a prime example of a Skinnerian concept that can have great value in one's life (even if certain other aspects of Skinner's approach aren't accepted).

Positive reinforcement seems very simple. In fact, it seems so simple that often it is overlooked. We frequently don't provide reinforcement when we should. Many times we "expect" individuals to behave well and therefore fail to positively reinforce their good behaviors when they occur. This is true in teacher-student, parent-child, supervisor-worker, wife-husband, friend-friend, and other types of relationships. We don't notice or we overlook good behavior, as though somehow it is supposed to occur without any external influence. This goes back to the traditional idea that people should behave well because of inner motivations, that is, they should "want" to be good, they should have the "desire" to behave well, and they should have enough "common sense" to know what the correct behaviors are. I still find myself falling into this type of thinking occasionally, but it's nonproductive. As much as we may wish that others would "instinctively" be nice, considerate, and so forth, their behaviors are influenced by their past and present circumstances. If those circumstances don't include positive reinforcement for desirable behaviors, such behaviors are unlikely to occur.

An interesting aspect of human interactions is that we often are more likely to show appreciation when strangers or casual acquaintances are courteous or helpful, than we are when those close to us behave in these ways. We tend to grow lax in acknowledging the positive actions of those whom we know well. This eventually can lead to poor relationships, with few mutually reinforcing interactions. The technical explanation for this includes *intermittent reinforcement* (for details, see chapter 3). The considerate and loving behaviors involved in intimate relationships are maintained by irregular reinforcements; in other words, sometimes these behaviors are acknowledged, and appreciation is shown, and sometimes they aren't. This is fine to a certain extent, but serious problems arise when *many* such behaviors are ignored, causing them to occur very infrequently or to stop completely (technically, *extinction* occurs). Obviously, when this happens the relationship is in bad shape.

Skinner's writings are helpful here. They can change our behaviors and make our relationships more satisfying, because they point out the importance of positive reinforcement. Since studying Skinnerian psychology, I find myself more likely to regularly express appreciation for the things those close to me do to make my life more comfortable and enjoyable (however, not being perfect, I still let too many opportunities to reinforce these behaviors slip by). Expressing appreciation (and this doesn't mean "wearing it out" by saying "thank you," or by going into dramatic gestures, for every little thing) has two important outcomes: (1) it makes it more likely that nice things will continue to be done for me (thereby making me feel good), and (2) it makes the persons doing them feel good. Of course, I too am susceptible to positive reinforcement, so my behaviors also are affected by the appreciation I receive from others. In short, reinforcement works in both directions. I believe that Skinner is right when he says that our behaviors are strongly determined by our environmental conditions, and the best conditions are those in which positive reinforcement prevails.

It's easy to believe that intimate relationships transcend mundane considerations such as positive reinforcement, but I'm convinced that these relationships can be explained (in large part, if not totally) by referring to this concept. In our society, "love" frequently is discussed in almost mystical terms. The expression "love is blind" indicates that lovers are not aware of each other's faults or shortcomings, but unfortunately this usually fades with time. New lovers often heap positive reinforcers (compliments, attention, affection, gifts, sex, etc.) on each other. This mutual reinforcement results in feelings of being "deeply in love." When such situations deteriorate, perhaps it is because there is too much initial reinforcement, in the sense that when other activities (working, seeing friends, playing sports, pursuing hobbies, or whatever) are given attention, the disruption of intense mutual reinforcement is disturbing to one person or the other.

It's next to impossible for one person to be the sole source of positive reinforcement for another, and though romances may begin in that vein, other reinforcers eventually influence the behaviors of those involved. If this occurs unevenly (one person finds more outside reinforcers than the other) problems seem especially likely to arise. One of the partners may start complaining or making threats (thereby introducing aversive stimuli), causing the other to begin avoiding the relationship (which will be negatively reinforcing—see chapter 3) and perhaps find more and more reinforcement elsewhere. And so it goes, until the relationship breaks up or is characterized by bickering and arguing (or, because both breaking up and arguing can be very aversive, the couple may stay together, but spend their time with each other in silence or in talking about trivial, noncontroversial subjects).

Skinner's suggestions are relevant to these situations. When we recognize the effects of positive reinforcement, we are less likely to "fall blindly into love" and more likely to adjust our responses so that we maintain mutually beneficial relationships for longer periods of time. Initially, it seems to me, it's important to realize that positive reinforcers are found in many different types of situations and activities, and not to behave as though one situation (or one person) will supply *everything*. Such behaviors too often lead to failure (perhaps accounting partly for the high divorce rate that exists), with accompanying feelings of disappointment, guilt, resentment, anger, and so on (remember, Skinner agrees that unpleasant feelings can arise from certain environmental events, and certainly the deterioration of a relationship would classify as such an event).

What I have just suggested in no way rules out feelings of love. When we interact with persons in certain intimate and reinforcing ways, we will feel reactions that we have learned to label as "love." This doesn't need to be continually analyzed in detail or spoiled by cold objectivity. In other words, it's fine to relax and enjoy "being in love," but it seems wise to try to maintain a good thing, and positive reinforcement plays an important role.

At the start of a relationship, behaving as though the *only* positive reinforcements in life will come from one's lover is almost certain to lead to problems, very likely in the form of one or both partners eventually using aversive methods of control to try to maintain the continual flow of reinforcers. On the other hand, lovers who regularly behave in positively reinforcing ways toward each other (but not to the point where each partner is the other's only source of reinforcement) will experience more enduring satisfactions. With some consistency, we should acknowledge those behaviors that are important in our relationships. If we don't, they may gradually disappear (extinguish). Then we will be left wondering, "What happened between us? It used to be so great, and now it's gone." It's easy to think that good, lasting relationships happen "naturally," but partners who continue to recognize and appreciate each other's considerate and loving behaviors (and avoid trying to control each other's behavior by aversive threats or punishments) are tipping the scales heavily in their favor.

Intimate relationships, of course, are not the only interpersonal situations to which positive reinforcement applies. It is relevant whenever persons interact. As Skinner has made clear, there's a lot of aversive and punitive control in the world and too little appropriate use of positive reinforcement. Threats, subtle or direct, are used frequently to get people to do what is expected of them. As indicated above, this can happen under circumstances in which desirable behaviors consistently are ignored until they eventually drop to near zero in occurrence, whereupon threats are used to try to restore the behaviors.

Some years ago I worked in a factory alongside a new employee who was fairly effective at his job. The supervisor, for some reason unknown to me, never acknowledged this man's work. In fact, he generally ignored him completely. Gradually the man's performance level decreased to a pathetic level (in technical terms, it *extinguished*). At this point, the supervisor started harassing him and threatened to have him transferred to another, more undesirable, department (the use of *aversive control*). The worker then stepped up his production (which was *negatively reinforced*, that is, this behavior was strengthened because it removed the aversive stimuli of harassment and threats). As is common with aversive control, however, it not only had the immediate desirable effect of increasing the worker's output, but it also had some undesirable effects: He had difficulties learning new tasks, he complained bitterly to his co-workers about the supervisor and the job, he started having physical ailments, and eventually he quit the job.

My assessment of this man was that he had the basic abilities to do an effective job (as he proved during his first few weeks at work). However, the total absence of positive feedback about his performance (lack of reinforcing comments from the supervisor) gradually led to a situation involving aversive control, and this paved the way to his leaving the job in order to escape the aversive conditions. I've often thought about this case: A little positive reinforcement would have gone a long way. I also believe that it is a common example. Workers, as well as persons in other kinds of situations, often do not get sufficient positive feedback about their good performance, and therefore don't function nearly as effectively as they could. However, before putting blame on supervisors or others who are in charge, remember that they too are affected by their circumstances. The whole system may need to be evaluated in order to see why aversive control is used so often.

Before leaving the topic of positive reinforcement in interpersonal relations, a few words of caution are in order. It isn't sufficient simply to supply more reinforcers to those with whom we interact. They must be applied in a discriminating way if they are to have beneficial results. Positive reinforcers strengthen the behaviors they follow, so we should be sure that a behavior is desirable before we reinforce it. Parents who give in to their childrens' temper tantrums, employees who yield to unfair requests from their employers, wives or husbands who give up valued activities because of complaining spouses, teachers who approve the inadequate work of their students, and those who go along with the inconsiderate demands of their friends, are examples of persons who are positively reinforcing undesirable behaviors. We need more positive reinforcement in the world, but it should be applied discriminately. We already have too much inappropriate positive reinforcement.

When it is appropriate to use positive reinforcement, it must be remembered that is is essential to find something that will work as a positive reinforcer. Occasionally, attempts to reinforce good behavior with the usual rewards, such as attention, affection, praise, gifts, and so on, do not work. Although in many cases these are effective reinforcers, in some cases they fail to strengthen desired behavior. When this happens, they cannot be considered reinforcers, and the search for something more effective must continue. What is actually a reinforcer may depend on the particular person, behavior, and/or occasion.

ASSIGNING BLAME

Being influenced by Skinner's writings is likely to change, at least to some extent, the tendency to blame others for their behaviors, however annoying or harmful they may be. When we blame others, we censure, accuse, or hold them responsible for their actions. In everyday life, it's difficult not to do this. This practice is part of our cultural tradition and most of us have learned it well. Sometimes it's effective in curtailing undesirable behaviors, at least temporarily. To avoid further blame, persons may avoid repeating condemned behaviors. Also, the *threat* of blame sometimes gets people to behave "properly". The basic message is: "If you don't do as expected, you will be considered irresponsible and held to blame."

Despite the fact that punitive or aversive methods of control (such as assigning blame) are sometimes effective, they have serious drawbacks. As discussed before, their outcomes are unpredictable. Will the person do as requested, or will he or she leave the situation? Will the person avoid the situation in the future? Will the person counterattack? Will the person complain bitterly or behave in other disturbing ways? Even if the person does as requested in the presence of the controller, will he or she continue to do so when the controller isn't around? Besides raising these questions, punishment and aversive control produce undesirable emotional responses in those on whom they are used. Persons certainly are not happy or satisfied when they are being controlled by such methods.

The point is this: Even if it's assumed that individuals are responsible for their behaviors, and therefore assigning blame for objectionable actions is justified, it doesn't consistently work well and it causes ill feelings. There is ample evidence for the long-range failure of this approach. Despite our extensive history of blaming people for all sorts of undesirable activities, these activities are still common.

In Skinner's approach, assigning blame is inappropriate, because there is no personal responsibility in the traditional sense. When someone does something annoying or harmful, the question is "What's wrong with the person's environment or environmental history?" and not "What's wrong with him (her)?" This way of looking at things requires a major shift from our usual viewpoint. Also, it sometimes can be a very burdensome approach, because the critical environmental conditions may be hard to find and may be difficult, or even impossible, to change. Being a radical behaviorist often requires great persistence. It's often much quicker and simpler to say "It's your fault. You're to blame." (Of course, when critical environmental factors can't be found and controlled in order to change offensive behaviors, then it is very likely that punitive or aversive methods such as assigning blame will be used.)

My own efforts to find environmental causes of behaviors have been reinforced sufficiently to keep me going in that direction, although I sometimes catch myself blaming others for certain actions (especially when I'm not reinforced for other responses). Blame basically is useless, except perhaps as a temporary measure when other, more effective, methods are unavailable. If the environmental factors causing the offensive behaviors (factors such as reinforcement for offensive behaviors or lack of opportunities and reinforcement for more desirable behaviors) can be found and changed, the behaviors that are of concern will change. If these environmental conditions can't be altered, then blame still is unlikely to do an adequate job. It may even aggravate the problem (this is especially true when alternative, desirable behaviors are unlikely to be emitted by the offending individual, so that there are no improved behaviors to positively reinforce). Still, it must be remembered that blaming is a likely response when other methods of control can't be applied effectively.

How can more people be convinced of the inefficiency of assigning blame and encouraged to seek out and change environmental conditions? When this happens, I believe that it occurs for reasons that also can be explained by Skinnerian psychology. That is, if individuals read Skinner's writings (or some other behavioristic information, such as that contained in this book) and are changed by what they discover, they may then apply the approach in their own lives. If the approach is effective (reinforcing), it will continue to be used.

Important practical questions arise if it's assumed that personal responsibility and blame are not applicable to human behavior: "What should be done with persons who are dangerous to others or who carry out criminal activities? Should such persons be allowed to run around free until we find the environmental causes of their behaviors and change those causes?" Though arguments *for* environmental determinism, and *against* personal responsibility and blame, might seem to imply an excessively lenient approach to dangerous or criminal actions, such is not necessarily the case. For practical reasons of public safety and well-being, persons who behave in these ways may have to be institutionalized or imprisoned, but *not* for revenge or to make them "pay for their crimes."

At the present, despite the fact that I believe the environment is the key to both "right" and "wrong" behaviors (with the possible exception of persons who act in disruptive or criminal ways because of brain damage or other neurophysiological abnormalities), I realize that we don't know all of the critical environmental determinants or how to change them. Skinner has put us on the correct track, but much work remains before we have complete, detailed answers. In the meantime, until we can construct a society in which harmful behaviors are much less prevalent and until we know with certainty how to change such behaviors when they occur, it will be necessary to provide the safeguard of confining certain individuals. The essential point, however, is that we should *not* behave as though confinement is giving the person "what he or she deserves." It should be considered a practical step to protect the public, until the better solution of improving the social environment reaches the point where harmful behaviors no longer occur.

There is a great difference between confinement as punishment and confinement as a practical matter (though admittedly, to the institutionalized or imprisoned person, the difference might not be clear). In the former case, we continue to hold individuals personally responsible for their actions and to blame them when they fail to act appropriately. This approach has been used for a very long time with highly questionable results. In the latter case, we continue to seek out the environmental causes of behavior, to change these factors to promote better behaviors, and to develop methods for modifying undesirable or harmful behaviors when they occur. This type of approach has been used with considerable success during recent years by behaviorists working in many different types of settings (clinical, school, family, institutional, and so on), to modify a wide variety of behaviors. If we follow Skinner's advice, we'll work toward much broader applications. Assigning blame, and holding individuals personally responsible for what they do, can inhibit progress in this direction. To the extent that our time and efforts are taken up with blaming, accusing, censuring, and so on, we will have less time and energy to examine the environmental determinants of behavior.

SELF-BLAME
AND "TURNING INWARD"

Along with our strong cultural tradition of *blaming others*, we have a powerful tendency to blame ourselves for "improper behaviors" or "signs of weakness." Here is another area in which I've been influenced by Skinner. Though I still accuse myself at times of being stupid, irrational, inconsistent, and so on, I do relatively little of this self-condemnation compared to times past.

I've found that blaming myself gets me nowhere. It may have

the reinforcing effect of reducing the condemnation of others (if we blame ourselves, others sometimes are less likely to add their blame to the situation), but it doesn't change the basic environmental causes of stupid, irrational, or inconsistent behaviors. I, as well as others, do these things because of circumstances such as inadequate learning (which causes us to behave "stupidly"), the presence of aversive conditions (which we escape or avoid, often in "irrational" ways), and the existence of conflicting consequences of our behaviors (if a particular behavior has been both reinforced and punished, we are apt to behave "inconsistently"). These are the types of causes that I now tend to look for when my own behaviors disturb me.

Focusing on "What's wrong with the environment and how can it be changed?" rather than "What's wrong with me?" can often have beneficial and long-lasting effects. However, there are potential problems. As indicated before, critical environmental factors (such as subtle aversive conditions or lack of appropriate reinforcements) may be difficult to find, and once found, difficult to change. Obvious environmental conditions aren't necessarily changed easily either. For example, a woman who stops blaming herself for being depressed and starts looking for external reasons, might quickly find causes in a boring job, an irritable or sarcastic employer, or an extremely jealous husband. Changing such causes, however clear they may be, can be a tough process.

Given these problems, a person attempting to take a behavioristic approach to life may "give up" (extinguish) before she or he has had the chance to see its effectiveness (that is, before reinforcement occurs). In order to prevent the extinction of attempts to locate and change important environmental conditions, it's essential to receive some reinforcement for these efforts. Therefore, if you decide to give the Skinnerian approach a try, don't tackle the biggest (and perhaps most difficult) situations first. There usually are minor changes that can be made at the start, at least some of which are likely to be effective (reinforcing). These positive consequences help ensure that the approach will be continued.

The depressed woman just mentioned perhaps should begin by making minor changes. Maybe she could change something about the way she does her job (for example, altering the sequence of tasks) or the physical setting in which she works (perhaps a furniture rearrangement or some minor decorating). Self-monitoring might help: Keeping track of work output sometimes is reinforcing in itself and sometimes can help things go more smoothly. A chart showing work progress provides visible evidence that something is being accomplished and also can indicate the times during the work day when efficiency usually drops off (these may be times when breaks should be scheduled). She could try to do something enjoyable during her lunch hour (reading, a quick shopping trip, eating with a friend, etc.). Some different ways of relating to her employer or husband could be attempted (perhaps a bit more assertiveness, or a bit less, depending on the circumstances). Also, she might ask them to make some small changes (for example, to give her more opportunity to try things on her own before they give advice.)

These particular suggestions might not work for everyone (actual change programs need to be tailored to the individual case), but I am simply trying to indicate that there are constructive alternatives to self-blame (or blaming others) when one has problems. By proceeding as suggested, the woman probably would do at least some things that would have positive effects (she then would be likely to continue making changes, and also her mood would be likely to change for the better.) At some point, a relatively dramatic change such as quitting her job, confronting her employer, or divorcing her husband might occur. On the other hand, less drastic changes might be sufficiently reinforcing (and her depression alleviated) so that more extreme actions would never occur.

Of course, our hypothetical woman could continue to blame herself for her depressed condition and turn inward, focusing intensely on her depressed feelings, examining in detail her "inner self," and ruminating about her "personality flaws." The unfortunate aspect of this, besides the continued unpleasant emotions that she would experience, is that it would detract from the direct alteration of her circumstances and behaviors. A basic question is: "Excluding certain changes induced by drugs, illnesses, and other such chemical or physiological conditions, are our feelings or states of mind (depression, anxiety, low self-esteem, etc.) likely to change unless environmental and behavioral changes occur?"

I agree with Skinner's suggestion that they are not. A behavioristic approach begins where other approaches indirectly end up in the long run: with behaviors and the factors that control them. Evaluating and altering situations, behaviors, and behavioral consequences, rather than introspection, are essential for overcoming dreary personal situations. Skinner suggests that we're wasting our time when we don't go directly to the modification of our behaviors through environmental control.

We often believe that we have "gotten over a bad mood" or "straightened out our thinking" by turning inward and engaging in self-examination. Though that may *seem* to be the case, it's quite possible (as Skinnerian psychology suggests) that while we are introspecting, external behavioral and environmental changes are occurring, which affects our emotions and thoughts. For example, an athlete who performs poorly during an important sporting event may develop strong feelings of inadequacy and inferiority. A year later, he may be performing at a higher level than ever before. When asked about this, he might say: "I did a lot of thinking and self-examination during this past year. I thought about my motives and my bad feelings. I feel I've found some answers inside myself. I'm not putting myself down anymore and I've got the will to win. I'm doing pretty well now."

We're accustomed to hearing these kinds of explanations, (not only from athletes, but from people in general) and we tend to accept them as the real explanations for improved behaviors and feelings. A behavioristic analysis, however, might reveal other factors. To use the example of the athlete, during the past year he may have changed his diet and training techniques, thereby upgrading his performance. Then he may have entered and won several competitions, resulting in consistent improvements in ability and state of mind. Also, he may have had a coach, close friends, relatives, and others who encouraged and praised his efforts. Luckily for him, these conditions prevailed at the same time that he was "focusing inward" and "self-examining;" if he had engaged only in introspective behaviors, it's unlikely that he would have finished the year in winning form.

In short, it is likely that changed circumstances and behaviors account for this athlete's high performance level *and* his good feelings about himself. As he sees it, and as many people would believe, he analyzed his inner states, they changed, and therefore his performance improved. The difference between this explanation and a behavioristic one, is that the former emphasizes the changing of feelings which then cause behavioral changes. The latter suggests that changed environmental conditions (such as a different diet and training program, a series of successes, and the support of those close to him) caused his improved performance and better emotional condition.

But, it might be asked, "Didn't he make up his mind to change his diet and his training procedures? Wasn't that an act of will?" Perhaps, but not according to a behavioristic analysis, which suggests that envirnomental events (such as a losing performance) resulted in behaviors (changing his diet and training methods) that would change the aversive condition of "losing." Simply put, the events that occurred in the athlete's life, not some "choice" or "decision," determined his behaviors. "How come he came back to win, while others might have given up?" The answer to this question, from a behavioristic perspective, would involve a detailed look at the circumstances surrounding each individual case. Maybe the athlete who "gives up" doesn't have the support of intimate friends, doesn't discover improved techniques, or has several critical defeats in a row because of stiff competition. Also, events earlier in a person's life can be key factors.

As much as we would like to believe that positive changes in behaviors are due to "making up our minds" or "showing will power," I think that Skinner's suggestions are vital: Environmental circumstances control our behaviors and we ought to focus on beneficially altering these circumstances. Self-blame, and accompanying introspective analyses, are likely to distract from going directly to the significant environmental determinants of our behaviors.

Each person has to look at his or her own environment and behaviors in order to know what to modify. For example, smokers and overeaters (some of whom do a lot of self-blaming for their indulgences) might be able to reduce consumption by avoiding certain situations in which those behaviors are especially likely to occur, and may cut down even further by doing things that are incompatible with smoking or overeating (such as exercising or playing sports). Another aid is to set up the situation so that some reinforcement (taking a short trip, buying something special, going to a movie, etc.) is dependent on staying away from cigarettes or fattening foods for a specified length of time. All of these methods involve changes in environmental factors.

For heavy smokers or those with serious weight problems, such methods may need to be supplemented by professional help in planning and carrying out behavior-modification programs. In any case, the emphasis should shift from self-blame to constructive alterations of environmental conditions (that is, staying away from situations in which "temptations" are especially likely, putting oneself in circumstances where incompatible behaviors are required, setting things up so that more desirable behaviors get reinforced, and so on).

Self-blame is far less likely to have positive results than are these types of measures. A behavioristic motto could be: "Stop blaming yourself and start changing your environment." Remember, though, if a behavior-modification program is to continue being used, using it *must* be reinforced. Small changes that are likely to have at least a minor positive effect can maintain the approach, as you move toward the solution of larger problems.[1]

To finish off the topics of self-blame and the inefficiency of

[1] See footnote 2 in Chapter 5 for references to self-modification books.

focusing inward to find answers to our problems, let's look again at the situation mentioned earlier in this chapter: the deterioration of an intimate relationship. When things start going wrong, typically there are self-doubts and feelings of anxiety, guilt, depression, and so on. Self-accusations are common, with one or both individuals thinking: "What's wrong with me? Is it my fault? Did I bring this about? Am I really unstable? Do I know what I want?" This can go on and on.

We sometimes assume that if these questions are thought about long and hard enough, and if our feelings are examined in sufficient detail and with sufficient intensity, answers to our problems will emerge. However, Skinner's approach suggests that we are "putting the cart before the horse" when we expect our feelings to explain what's going on in our lives. Instead, if we look closely at existing conditions and the positive and negative outcomes of our behaviors, we'll find out not only why we are behaving as we are, but also why we feel as we do. If there are subtle or hidden meanings to be discovered, these meanings are less likely to be found by intense introspection and tireless self-examination than by careful observations of the environmental circumstances and events affecting us.

Rather than blaming ourselves and engaging in persistent self-analyses when our relationships are in trouble, it is better to focus on questions such as: "What specifically is it that each of us does that is aversive to the other (causing him or her to escape or avoid the relationship)? Do we show appreciation (give reinforcement) when one does something that the other likes? Do we ignore (extinguish) each other at times when we should be paying attention (giving reinforcement) to one another? What circumstances serve to strengthen (reinforce) our intimate and loving behaviors? What circumstances serve to suppress (punish) such behaviors? What positive outcomes (reinforcers) are we getting by staying together? What positive outcomes exist outside the relationship?"

These types of questions direct attention to the actual sources of many problems. The answers relate to events that are more external and objective than what happens to be going on inside our heads at a particular time (that is, the complex mixture of feelings and thoughts that are resulting from what is happening to us). Therefore, the answers provide a more solid basis for evaluating the good and bad points of the relationship and, most importantly, suggest specific ways in which changes for the better might be made. They provide something concrete with which to work. Does this mean that the relationship will be saved? Not necessarily. It depends on the actual positive reinforcers and aversive conditions that exist, and the effects of the behavioral changes that are made. In cases when more reinforcements occur elsewhere, or when aversive conditions cannot be changed significantly, the relationship is not likely to survive.

What about the breakup of a relationship and the accompanying feelings of inadequacy, insecurity, anger, and so on? I believe that the same analysis as above applies here. You can dwell on these feelings or you can focus on the conditions that produce them. If you do the latter, then you are more likely to be able to change conditions so that you experience better feelings. Using a personal example, my immediate response to the breakup of my marriage was one of loss, loneliness, and doubts about the future. Fortunately, events occurred to prevent me from continuing a lot of wasteful and depressing introspection and self-examination (which I had done much of before the separation). After our separation, I began a short, but reinforcing, new relationship, intensified some old friendships and started some new ones, and got heavily involved in work and my university graduate studies. (I feel very lucky, in retrospect. This was years before I developed a strong interest in Skinnerian psychology, so I wasn't "planning" my behaviors according to a behavioristic model. It just so happened that I was fortunate. My environment was one which was rich in potential reinforcers, and therefore new behaviors were relatively easily shaped and maintained.)

Because of this and many later experiences (not the least of which has been Skinner's influence) I have come to believe that environmental events dominate our feelings. More and more I find myself in agreement with the Skinnerian idea that *feelings are caused, rather than being causes,* and therefore it doesn't pay to keep searching within ourselves for answers to our problems. When we are depressed, anxious, or have other unpleasant emotions, we should look for the relevant environmental conditions (such as lack of positive reinforcement for our behaviors or the presence of aversive stimuli) that produce these feelings. It is by altering these conditions that we are most likely to get rid of negative feelings and produce positive ones.

THE IMMEDIACY AND IMPORTANCE OF FEELINGS

Technically, feelings can be considered as stimuli that arise within our bodies. They are related to various environmental events, such as receiving reinforcement or punishment for some behavior. We learn during the socialization process to label these stimuli as "joy," "anxiety," "sadness," and so on, depending on the circumstances under which they occur.

Why do we have strong tendencies to assign major importance to our feelings and to ruminate about them, instead of paying more attention to the objective environmental conditions and behaviors of which they are products? A significant reason is because they are so immediate. Feelings are "right here," while objective events that are reinforcing or punishing are happening "out there." There are many subtle behaviors, reinforcements, and punishments that are especially likely to escape our attention as we focus on our feelings. We often get taken up with the feelings themselves, which of course is very nice when they are pleasurable. However, when a feeling is negative, or when we would like to reproduce the conditions that give us positive feelings, it is the environment that needs investigating. It's not unusual to hear someone say something like: "I was feeling so great, and then things just seemed to fall apart. I really feel down, and

I'm not sure what to do." In such cases, a healthy dose of behaviorism can be helpful.

How does someone become a Skinnerian-type behaviorist, focusing on objective behaviors and consequences? In the same way that other behaviors are learned: through experience. As indicated earlier, if reading this book causes you to focus more on your environment, and this way of behaving is then reinforced (perhaps by alleviating some problem), you'll be on the road to becoming more behavioristic. An essential aspect of this approach involves "testing out" behaviors. I've often found it more efficient and effective to get direct feedback from the environment by actually doing something, rather than continuing to ponder what the outcomes of behaviors *might* be. Sometimes, of course, the behavioral consequences are negative, but that isn't necessarily bad. In order to avoid such consequences again, I do something else, which might be reinforced. What I'm suggesting is that more action and less unproductive ruminating (as occurs, for example, when we have had no experiences that allow us to predict consequences) is generally in order. Though I still ruminate too much, I've been weaned away from that approach to a considerable extent by the reinforcements I've gotten for being more behavior-oriented.

I want to make it clear that what I've said about feelings is not meant to negate their significance. We live with them, and it's important to most of us that we experience positive ones. A Skinnerian analysis, it seems to me, makes it more likely that we will be able to live fully and enjoyably. By understanding how our behaviors, their consequences, and surrounding conditions affect our feelings, we can maximize constructive behaviors and positive emotions.

It's obvious that many persons have a great deal of trouble clearly identifying what they are feeling at various times; they also often seem unsure of what actions to take. These confused feelings and uncertain behaviors can result from inconsistent histories of reinforcement. For example, if in a particular type of situation a behavior results in punishment at one time and reinforcement the next, the individual is bound to experience confused feelings and act in uncertain ways.

A vivid and distressing example of this occurred many years ago when I was sitting in a laundromat, waiting for my clothes to finish drying. A woman was there with her son, who looked about five or six years old. The boy would cling to his mother for a time, and she would then begin to tell him to stop acting like a baby and eventually slap him several times, causing him to retreat to a corner of the laundromat. She would then call him back, hug him, and tell him that he was a good boy. After a few minutes of the boy's clinging to her, the cycle would start again: more chastising by the mother, several slaps, the boy retreating, the mother calling him back, and so on. I wondered about this boy's prospects. If this kind of treatment was common in his life, how would he ever develop a set of consistent feelings and behaviors? Mood swings and indecisive actions would seem to be predictable outcomes of his experiences with his erratic mother.

Though this type of dramatically inconsistent experience probably isn't common, more subtle inconsistencies are part of the lives of most of us and cause varying degrees of confused feelings and uncertainties in behavior. We are fortunate when we have enough consistency of positive reinforcement in our everyday lives—in social situations, at home, on the job, and so on—to develop fairly well-defined feelings and confident behaviors. Some persons, however, may have to seek out special situations, such as psychotherapy or behavior therapy, in order to straighten our their feelings and behaviors.

Though the methods used by various therapists differ, a common aspect of many approaches is to provide a consistent, predictable environment within the therapy setting. This type of environment may be precisely what many troubled persons need, since it can serve to steady confused feelings and cause individuals to become increasingly sure of what they are experiencing from within, while also producing more certain behaviors. Both feelings *and* behaviors will be affected if the therapy is successful. (Remember, however, that a behavioristic analysis does not suggest that it is changed feelings that are of importance in bringing about behavioral changes. Contrary to what many therapists believe, radical behaviorists maintain that the environment ultimately exerts control. The "environment" in this case includes the therapeutic setting, the therapist's behaviors, the consequences of the client's behaviors, and so on—these environmental factors are related to whatever improvements there are in the client's emotional states and overt behavioral responses.)

What I am suggesting here is consistent with Skinner's suggestion that feelings are effects, not causes. I believe that we need to experience fairly consistent feelings (effects) for similar behaviors in similar circumstances in order to be "well-adjusted." Some degree of emotional stability is essential to our well-being, and this stability results from reasonably consistent histories of reinforcement. Putting this in simple terms, we need reliable love and affection from those with whom we are intimately involved, reliable reinforcements for our work output, and so on. There is nothing new in these recommendations. However, from a Skinnerian perspective, we can see even more clearly that what determines consistent behaviors and emotional states are consistent consequences and conditions provided by our environments. Erratic environments tend to produce persons who are erratic in their behaviors and feelings.

Skinner's radical behaviorism casts a clear, and often unique, light on many aspects of everyday situations and behaviors. Also, it points out factors that should be obvious to us, but which we often ignore. As detailed in the previous pages, it has helped me to focus on (1) the importance of positive reinforcement in interpersonal relations, (2) the long-range futility of blaming others for their annoying, disruptive, or harmful behaviors, (3) the inefficiency of self-blame and intensive self-analysis, and (4) the role that feelings play in our lives. Much of this chapter consists of my own elaborations on Skinner's ideas, but I believe I've remained within his behavioristic framework.

TEN

CONCLUDING COMMENTS

Perhaps the aspects of Skinnerian psychology that most often are found disturbing are its radical determinism and its emphasis on control. Many persons seem unable to get past these issues to look objectively at other features of Skinner's approach. They simply can't accept that our behaviors are determined and continually controlled by genetic and environmental factors. Admittedly, these are hard pills to swallow. We feel free and able to make choices and decisions about our lives (at least sometimes) and therefore it just doesn't seem to make sense to say that we have no real freedom and are controlled all of the time.

I've often thought about the implications of radical determinism and they are mind-boggling. Although it may represent the way things really are (and essentially I believe that it's true), most of us can't live on a day-to-day basis with this philosophy constantly in mind. To some extent, I sympathize with Skinner's critics who suggest that a radically deterministic view makes nonsense of our lives. If ultimate control rests in genetic and environmental factors, and we are only "loci" for these factors, what's the use of trying to improve ourselves or the world—our fates, as well as the fate of society, are sealed by fortunate or unfortunate genetic structures and environmental circumstances.

If Skinner's research and writings, as well as the activities of all of us, are determined by conditions that have nothing to do with personal choices and decisions, what meaning can anything have? Because of his genetic endowment and the consequences of various behaviors during his lifetime, Skinner is proposing certain ideas, and whether or not we accept his proposals is in turn determined by the genetic endowment and environmental circumstances of each of us. In other words, according to radical determinism, there is no point at which individual free choice enters into the process. To make a long story short, these considerations are nerve-wracking. Complete and constant agreement with radical determinism is impossible for most of us; it's simply too inconsistent with all we have learned as members of this society. (From a deterministic viewpoint, our genes and experiences have determined that we cannot "accept" a completely deterministic philosophy—as you can see, this is a very complicated business.)

Of course, if Skinner's type of determinism is rejected, then the rejector can be asked: "What else, other than genetic and environmental conditions, can determine behavior? If there is something beyond our bodies, with all their component parts, and the physical and social environments within which we function, what is it?" The answer could be "the human spirit," "the will of God," or some other such quality. However, these answers take us out of the naturalistic world of a science of human behavior. (Such qualities may or may not exist; in any case, naturalistic approaches to the study of human behavior cannot systematically take them into account.)

With regard to Skinner's deterministic position, a very important point must be made. It's one that is obvious but sometimes forgotten: His assumptions (as he himself has suggested) do not change what actually exists. Whether or not our lives are completely determined is not decided by what Skinner says. Either we live in a wholly determined system or we do not. If we do, it doesn't seem to affect the fact that we are capable of feeling as though we're free, nor does it change the feeling that our behaviors are meaningful. Therefore, do we have to be weighed down by heavy philosophical questions about "ultimate reality?" It seems to me that we can simply use Skinner's concepts and strive to change our environments so that productive and beneficial behaviors will increase and feelings of freedom will be enhanced.

When behavioristic procedures such as positive reinforcement are used and are effective, they continue to be used. The important step is getting beyond whatever aversive elements one finds in Skinnerian psychology, and I hope this book has the effect of making that happen. Even those who don't share Skinner's belief that behavior is completely determined by genetic and environmental factors can find beneficial applications of concepts such as positive reinforcement.

Although nowadays I spend little time concerning myself with whether or not we live in a completely determined world (a question that can't really be answered anyway), I do believe that the most effective way of understanding and changing behavior (my own and others') is to focus on environmental conditions. From this perspective, which is supported by a considerable amount of behavioral science research, much of what I hear and read about human behavior seems remarkably antiquated. Behaviorists have made great advances in recent years, and studies have shown that environmental changes in institutions, schools, businesses, family settings, and so on, can bring about beneficial behavioral changes. This often has been accomplished by planning situations in which appropriate positive reinforcement plays a greater role, while minimizing the use of punishment or aversive control. At the individual level also, persons have improved their own lives by applying behavioral procedures.

Despite these advances in knowledge about how environmental circumstances affect behavior, and the vast amount of behavioristic literature by Skinner and others, there still remain many persons who talk and write about human behavior as though the evidence and ideas of the behaviorists don't exist. (For example, it's doubtful that Freud himself, if he were still alive, would believe what he wrote in the 1920s and 1930s. Yet there are those today who hold orthodox Freudian ideas, or very similar ones, as the last words on human nature and behavior.)

Though Skinner's approach certainly has not yet proved to be the one and only possible explanation of behavior, it's surprising that its impressive advances have not been more widely recognized and acknowledged. For example, just by glancing through recent newspaper and magazine editorials and articles, it's easy to find comments similar to "the darkness in man's soul that corrupts his best intentions," "the destructive tendencies hidden deep within the human psyche, ready to burst forth at any moment," "the failing American character that is bringing us to the edge of national disaster," "the lack of morality and will power among our citizens," and so on.

The tone of certainty in many such statements makes it clear that the writers have been untouched by the possibility that environmental factors (rather than dark souls, hidden destructive tendencies, failing characters, or moral deficiencies) are primarily responsible for our problems. This focus on inner causes detracts from analyses of the effects of our political, economic, educational, legal, and other social institutions on our behaviors. Also, it directs our attention away from the multitude of environmental factors that affect our day-to-day lives on the job, at home, with our friends, etc.

Analyzing our environments and changing them so that positive reinforcement becomes the rule rather than the exception, and so that punitive and aversive controls are minimized, is a tough, time-consuming job. Perhaps that is a major reason why many people continue to explain human behavior in antiquated ways. It's quick and easy to blame our behavioral problems on something that is out of sight, such as a "dark soul" or a "moral deficiency." Also, we provide reinforcement for these types of explanations by agreeing with them: person number one says "The country is going to the dogs because no one has any moral fiber," and person number two replies "Yes, you're right. No one seems to care anymore." This is an easy interaction, and no long, drawn-out explanations of environmental influences are required. Of course, those influences also go unexamined and unchanged.

Reading and rereading Skinner's writings still remains of interest to me, despite the fact that I've been doing it for a number of years. One of the main reasons why I find his writings impressive is that his ideas, though sometimes extended considerably beyond his research findings, are nevertheless grounded in that research. He has, at some level, a sound basis for his suggestions. He spent many years in the experimental laboratory and many of his findings have been replicated in the real world outside of the laboratory. He is no "armchair philosopher."

Also, I continue to find nuggets of practical wisdom in Skinner's writings (which are reinforcers that keep me reading his books and articles). Recently, I came across an interesting commentary on happiness. In an article in the magazine *Human Nature* (March 1978, p. 91), he explains that it isn't the possession of goods, but rather the effective action that produces the goods, that makes us happy. He also suggests that we are mistaken when we believe that others will be happy if we simply give them good things. Their happiness is probable only if the things we give them enable them to take further action. The implication is that while acquiring things may make people happy, simply possessing them does not. This idea certainly is not brand new or completely unique, but it is one that is worth being reminded of. It is easy to slip into believing that "once I get what I want (money, a good job, an expensive house, or whatever), I will be happy." As many persons have found out, getting these things may be much more fun than having them, especially when they fail to lead to other effective and fulfilling behaviors.

Finally, Skinnerian behaviorism makes me optimistic. It's an approach that allows us to escape the weight of the often gloomy history of humankind. Each new generation (and, for that matter, each individual) offers renewed possibilities for the improvement of civilization. We aren't stuck with our current problems; we can improve; the status quo is not what we have to live with. Also, radical behaviorism offers a practical program for change, based on observable conditions and events. All in all, I believe that Skinner has made a major contribution to the betterment of an ailing world. Best of all, his procedures and ideas can be used even by those who have doubts about some of his underlying assumptions. We don't have to become "disciples" in order to apply his suggestions and observe the effects.

ANNOTATED
REFERENCES

PRIMARY REFERENCES
(main sources used for this book)

Evans, Richard I., *B. F. Skinner: The Man and His Ideas*. New York: E. P. Dutton, 1968. A book-length interview, in which Skinner informally answers questions about Freud, aversive versus positive methods of control, education, the role of theories, misunderstandings and misinterpretations of his approach, and other topics.

Freud, Sigmund, *New Introductory Lectures on Psychoanalysis*. New York: W. W. Norton & Company, Inc., 1965. First published in 1933, this book contains seven lectures covering a variety of psychoanalytic topics.

————, *An Outline of Psycho-Analysis*. New York: W. W. Norton & Company, Inc., 1969. Originally published in 1940, this is Freud's last book. It is a concise overview of psychoanalytic theory.

Hall, Calvin S. *A Primer of Freudian Psychology*. New York: New American Library, 1954. A brief, widely known summary of Freudian theory.

Hall, Elizabeth, "Will Success Spoil B. F. Skinner?," *Psychology Today*, November 1972, pp. 65–72, 130. A wide-ranging interview, in which he talks about his work and its applications, the concepts of freedom and dignity, *Walden Two*, artistic behaviors, and more.

Hall, Mary Harrington, "An Interview with 'Mr. Behaviorist'— B. F. Skinner," *Psychology Today*, September 1967, pp. 21–23,

68–71. A lively interview in which he comments on religion, child-rearing, his critics, and other subjects.

Homans, George C., "A Conversation with B. F. Skinner, Psychologist," *Harvard Magazine*, July–August 1977, pp. 53–58. Homans, a distinguished Harvard sociologist, informally questions Skinner about his background, his scientific assumptions, teaching machines, *Walden Two*, the air crib that he used with his second daughter, and other interesting matters.

Rogers, Carl R. "A Theory of Therapy, Personality, and Interpersonal Relationships, as Developed in the Client-Centered Framework," in *Psychology: A Study of a Science* (vol. 3), pp. 184–256, ed. Sigmund Koch. New York: McGraw-Hill Book Company, 1959. The most complete and detailed presentation available of Rogers's theoretical assumptions.

———, *On Becoming a Person*. Boston: Houghton Mifflin Company, 1961. A wide-ranging collection of Rogers's papers, expressing his views on psychotherapy, research, and everyday-life situations.

———, "Toward a Science of the Person," in *Behaviorism and Phenomenology*, pp. 109–140, ed. T. W. Wann. Chicago: University of Chicago Press, 1964. Rogers presents his approach to the study of human behavior, which incorporates subjective, objective, and interpersonal knowledge.

———, *Freedom to Learn*. Columbus, Ohio: Charles E. Merrill Publishing Company, 1969. Rogers's views on teaching, learning, and the educational system.

———, and B. F. Skinner, "Some Issues Concerning the Control of Human Behavior," *Science*, 124, no. 3231 (November 30, 1956), 1057–1066. The well-known confrontation between Rogers and Skinner at a symposium held by the American Psychological Association. Each expressed his views, with the topic of how values emerge being a primary issue.

Skinner, B. F. *Walden Two*. New York: Macmillan, 1948. A novel about a utopian community based on the application of behavioral-science principles. Widely read and much discussed, this fictional work continues to stimulate, and often aggravate, its readers.

————, *Science and Human Behavior*. New York: Macmillan, 1953. Perhaps the best and most complete general introduction to his position. Covers a wide range of topics: the role of a science of human behavior, the analysis of behavior, self-control, thinking, social behavior, government and law, religion, psychotherapy, education, cultural design, and more.

————, "Teaching Machines," *Scientific American*, November 1961, pp. 90–102. Brief description of teaching machines and their advantages.

————, "Behaviorism at Fifty," *Science*, 140, no. 3570 (May 31, 1963), 951–958. A difficult article but worth studying; it states the case for a behavioristic philosophy of science. Deals in some detail with the topic of conscious experiencing.

————, "Autobiography," in *A History of Psychology in Autobiography* (vol. 5), pp. 385–413, eds. Edwin G. Boring and Gardner Lindzey. New York: Irvington Publishers, Inc., 1967. A brief, interesting overview of his life, beginning with his childhood in Susquehanna, Pennsylvania. Reveals major influences on his own behaviors.

————, *Beyond Freedom and Dignity*, New York: Alfred A. Knopf, 1971. A direct challenge to the traditional concepts of freedom and dignity. Calls for a technological approach to solving social problems, discusses alternatives to the widespread use of punishment, investigates values, suggests that cultural design be employed, asks "What Is Man?" and raises other important issues. Because of the publicity it received, this is his most controversial book.

————, *Cumulative Record: A Selection of Papers* (3rd. ed.). New York: Appleton-Century-Crofts, 1972. A collection of 48 articles covering various topics, including the concept of freedom, experimental method, education, psychoanalysis, psychoses, creativity, literary and verbal behavior, superstitious behavior, and theoretical matters.

————, "Answers for My Critics," in *Beyond the Punitive Society*, pp. 256–266, ed. Harvey Wheeler. San Francisco: W. H. Freeman and Company, 1973. An excellent short article that addresses major misunderstandings of his science of behavior and its uses.

————, "Humanism and Behaviorism," in *Without/Within: Behaviorism and Humanism*, pp. 47–53, ed. Floyd W. Matson. Monterey, Ca.: Brooks/Cole Publishing Company, 1973. A brief, clear statement of his position versus humanistic psychology's emphasis on the inner person.

————, *About Behaviorism*. New York: Alfred A. Knopf, 1974. A wide-ranging work, with a primary emphasis on clarifying his brand of behaviorism by correcting 20 common misconceptions. Among the issues are: the "world within the skin," innate behavior, verbal behavior, thinking, motivation and emotion, the self, and the question of control.

————, "The Steep and Thorny Way to a Science of Behavior," *American Psychologist*, 30, no. 1 (January 1975), 42–49. He briefly explains again his views on behavioral science, the role of feelings and "inner determinants," the importance of focusing on environmental factors, and other issues. The central theme is that we are being diverted from a scientific approach to human behavior.

————, *Particulars of My Life*. New York: Alfred A. Knopf, 1976. An interesting autobiographical account, it is the first volume in a planned three-volume series. Traces his development from childhood to his entry into the graduate psychology program at Harvard University. Includes fascinating details about growing up in a small northeastern town shortly after the turn of the century.

————, "Walden Two Revisited," in *Walden Two*, pp. v–xvi. New York: Macmillan, 1976 edition. A commentary on the background and relevance of his novel *Walden Two*, originally published in 1948. The commentary was written especially for this reissued edition.

————, "Why Don't We Use the Behavioral Sciences?," *Human Nature*, March 1978, pp. 86–92. An exceptionally clear and concise treatment of his views on the need for a behavioral-science approach to social problems and the uselessness of looking within the person for explanations of behavior.

TIME Staff, "Skinner's Utopia: Panacea, or Path to Hell?" *Time*, September 20, 1971, pp. 47–53. An interesting popular article on his work and life, and the controversies he has generated.

ADDITIONAL REFERENCES

Epstein, Robert, "A Listing of the Published Works of B. F. Skinner, with Notes and Comments," *Behaviorism*, 5, no. 1 (1977), 99–110.

Ferster, C. B., and B. F. Skinner, *Schedules of Reinforcement*. New York: Appleton-Century-Crofts, 1957. A detailed empirical examination of the effects of many different reinforcement patterns.

Holland, James G., and B. F. Skinner, *The Analysis of Behavior: A Program for Self-Instruction*. New York: McGraw-Hill, 1961. A programmed textbook that presents the basic terms and principles of the scientific analysis of behavior. As the authors point out: "This book is itself one application of the science."

Skinner, B. F., *The Behavior of Organisms*. New York: Appleton-Century-Crofts, 1938. His early experimental studies of behavior, using rats as subjects, are presented.

————, *Verbal Behavior*. New York: Appleton-Century-Crofts, 1957. An attempt to analyze language in terms of his operant approach.

————, *The Technology of Teaching.* New York: Appleton-Century-Crofts, 1968. The applications of his approach to problems of teaching and learning.

————, *Contingencies of Reinforcement: A Theoretical Analysis.* Englewood Cliffs, N. J.: Prentice-Hall, Inc., 1969. A restatement of his position on theoretical issues and the applications of behavioral science to cultural design.

————, "The Machine That Is Man," *Psychology Today*, April 1969, pp. 20–25, 60–63. An intriguing discussion of various views of the causes of human behavior, and the complexities of comparing humans and machines.

————, "Between Freedom and Despotism," *Psychology Today*, September 1977, pp. 80–91. A discussion of the importance of person-to-person positive reinforcement as a means of governing social behaviors.

————, *Reflections on Behaviorism and Society.* Englewood Cliffs, N. J.: Prentice-Hall, Inc., 1978. Contains 18 previously published articles on various socially relevant issues. A useful and informative preface serves as an overview of important points in the articles.

————, *The Shaping of a Behaviorist: Part Two of an Autobiography.* New York: Alfred A. Knopf, 1979. The second volume of a planned three-volume autobiography. The development of his ideas and research, and personal details of his life, are included.

For those interested in reading brief presentations of Skinner's approach and behavioral concepts, chapters in the following books are recommended:

Hall, Calvin S., and Gardner Lindzey, *Theories of Personality* (3rd ed.), pp. 637–680. New York: John Wiley and Sons, 1978.
Herganhahn, B. R., *An Introduction to Theories of Learning*, pp. 82–116. Englewood Cliffs, N. J.: Prentice-Hall, Inc., 1976.

Hilgard, Ernest R., and Gordon H. Bower, *Theories of Learning* (4th ed.), pp. 206–251. Englewood Cliffs, N.J.: Prentice-Hall, Inc., 1975.

Nye, Robert D., *Three Views of Man: Perspectives from Sigmund Freud, B. F. Skinner, and Carl Rogers*, pp. 35–80. Monterey, Ca.: Brooks/Cole Publishing Company, 1975.

INDEX